THE GOSPEL OF SELF

THE GOSPEL
OF SELF

How Pat Robertson Stole the Soul of
the GOP

TERRY
HEATON

OR Books
New York · London

Published by OR Books, New York and London
Visit our website at www.orbooks.com

All rights information: rights@orbooks.com

First printing 2019

Cataloging-in-Publication data is available from the Library of Congress.
A catalog record for this book is available from the British Library.

ISBN 978-1-949017-04-5 paperback
ISBN 978-1-949017-05-2 e-book

Text design by Under|Over. Typeset by Lapiz Digital Services.

Published for the book trade by OR Books in partnership with Counterpoint Press.
Distributed to the trade by Publishers Group West.

This is my story. It's one that begins with a quest to be more spiritual and ends with the realization that life is all about becoming more human. Along the way, I had a front-row seat as a participant in one of the most exciting, important, and, it turns out, potentially destructive social movements in human history.

How does one love something so much and yet hate it at the same time?

Table of Contents

Photo credit: Terry Heaton

(1983) On the set of *The 700 Club* on location at Universal Studios in Hollywood. The week in Hollywood—highlighted by a remarkable interview with Donna Summer—was a great team production and won awards in religious broadcasting competitions.

Photo credit: Terry Heaton

(1984) While all telethons were broadcast live, they still required rehearsal primarily for staff, camera blocking, and the control room. Here, Pat Robertson and co-host Ben Kinchlow play at the challenge board.

Photo credit: Terry Heaton

(1985) Chris Rylko was my sidekick and producer; this was as our picture was being taken for the newsletter. In my 45 years in television, Chris was the best pure producer I ever had at my side, and we're still friends today.

Photo credit: Terry Heaton

(1986) The jet purchased for Pat Robertson's campaign. Formerly owned by country music star Kenny Rogers, the tail number was NB88, which stood for "new beginnings 1988." Eight is the Biblical number for new beginnings.

One

The Seeds of Modern Discontent

*The modern conservative is engaged in one of man's
oldest exercises in moral philosophy; that is, the search
for a superior moral justification for selfishness.*
—John Kenneth Galbraith

The evangelist's message has always been self-centered, for it
preaches the gospel as a means to saving one's own ass from eternal
hellfire and damnation in the afterlife. Evangelical Christianity
has refined the message over the years and turned it today into
the means for blessings in this life as well. What was once a powerful motivator for overall good behavior in the community has
become a motivator for obtaining a better position in life, and it
has profoundly altered everything in our society from our politics to our treatment of our neighbors. I helped bring this about,
for I worked alongside one of the most influential evangelists of
modern history.

Marion Gordon "Pat" Robertson is a political animal that happens to be a Christian evangelist, broadcaster, and television personality. Political smarts flow through his veins as surely as the blood that sustains his body. He was born and raised in the midst of a powerful Virginia political family. His father, Absalom Willis Robertson, was a career conservative Democrat—a Dixiecrat of the Senator Robert Byrd ilk—serving in both the House and the Senate, and Pat was groomed to follow in his footsteps, attending the prestigious McDonogh Preparatory School before Washington and Lee University and eventually Yale Law School. He also served a stint in the Marine Corps as a first lieutenant.

Pat Robertson never passed the bar exam, but instead had a religious conversion. He went to New York Theological Seminary, receiving a Masters in Divinity in 1959. A year later he established the Christian Broadcasting Network (CBN) in Portsmouth, Virginia. He has built a massive television empire since and is one of the most controversial Evangelical Christians on TV, where he practices the charismatic "gifts of the spirit," including speaking in tongues and signs and wonders such as "healing." But the political animal continued to seek the surface throughout his television ministry, and this would play a huge role in my own life and in the political dynamics of the Republican Party, one that continues to this day.

When I worked with him in the 1980s, we practiced and promoted a brand of Charismatic Christianity that was seen as a breath of fresh air to a faith that had grown stale in every aspect, from its music to its preaching, and we worked long, hard hours to move hearts and souls in the way we felt was right. In so doing, we altered the course of political power in the United States, and it was as natural as our Christian calling. Taking positions on social issues formerly held by conservative Democrats, such as the sanctity of life, religious liberties, patriotism, family, school prayer, and respect for individualism and tradition, we spoke to primarily rural and suburban Christians on behalf of the Republican Party. We presented as Biblical mandates or "laws" economic views that catered to the haves of culture, teaching that being one of the haves was available for everybody. Our arguments and teachings helped move the GOP to the right on the political spectrum and created a following that continues to baffle even the smartest political analysts in the country who are confounded by how such people would act against their own best interests in giving power to Republicans.

Pat Robertson was a highly intelligent, articulate, well-read, creative, and brilliant man to work for. There wasn't a day that I didn't admire his ability to communicate via live television. The more prepared I was, the better he was able to perform. I was a willing participant in his social engineering, because I agreed with him that the world was going to hell, and I was proud to be at his side in trying to change that. And it didn't matter one bit to me that we crossed lines along the way. I was an experienced news executive, and I knew right from wrong when it came to journalism and the narratives of liberty.

I used that knowledge to bring our daily message right up to the edge of both ethics and the law without embarrassing ourselves. It turned out that my efforts could not protect us from what happened outside my purview. Many hands were involved in our political efforts, and it became evident that they weren't guided by the same principles we tried to apply to *The 700 Club*.

Moreover, there is a vast difference, I discovered, between what we believed and did as leaders and teachers, and what the students would do with what we taught them. This is why I don't fear conservative leaders in the world today, but I'm frightened to death by their followers. We broke the law. We stretched the truth. Why would we be surprised or complain if our followers did likewise? Our attempts to manage a political movement trapped us in the belief that God needed us and our work in order to accomplish change in the hearts of humankind. We organized human efforts to change, and that is an untenable position for those attempting publicly to do the work of God.

I do not know how to adequately justify this dichotomy in my own thinking and behavior during the time I helmed *The 700 Club*. Was I simply caught up in something that I couldn't handle? Was I naïve, because I was such a novice in the faith? Was my ego running the show, as I gave myself completely to the task of CBN? Perhaps it was none or all of the above, but I do know that we created—or at least played a major role in the creation of—the extreme Christian element that has dragged the Republican Party today to the edge of fascism. There is no zeal quite like that of religious zeal, for it comes with blinders to alternative views of reality. When this zeal is aimed at pleasing God Himself, it's impossible to negotiate or reason with it or its consequences.

And why should conservative leadership care as long as this group votes? Politics is a dirty, dirty business, as Pat discovered later with the tactics of his chief rival, George H.W. Bush. Trying to reform a culture through political means is vanity and a useless pursuit, and yet this was the consequential fruit of my work at CBN and *The 700 Club*. It may have been great television, but the internal price I paid, as you will later discover, almost brought about my total destruction as a man, a father, a believer in something bigger than myself, and as a professional observer.

Ronald Reagan was the President when I joined CBN, and there was a sense of revival in the air, for we had just come out of the decade of Vietnam, Watergate, and the Iranian hostage crisis. We had been floundering as a nation for more than a dozen years, since the assassinations of John F. Kennedy, Robert F. Kennedy, and Martin Luther King. By the early 1980s, people were suddenly hopeful that prosperity of all kinds would soon return to America, and I got deeply caught up in it. We were, after all, counterculture, and that fired my imagination and gave me strength, for we were in a position to actually make a difference in the lives of many.

Little did I—or anyone back then—realize how far off the rails we would run giving chase to a vision of God's will for Christians, the church, and the US as a whole. This is a profoundly difficult statement to make for me, who was so intimately involved in the process, but it is a truth nonetheless that must be examined without the blinders that accompany the fundamentalist regimen of certain Evangelical Christians. The stakes are simply too high for us and for our progeny to ignore the facts of what we did and mostly how we did it.

Fast-forward thirty years, and America is now a bitterly divided nation. It is as though a new civil war has emerged led by polar opposites on the political spectrum. All equilibrium seems lost, and we are awash in the chaos of division at every level. Add to this the remarkable technological advancements of the last fifteen years that have undercut the power of top-down communications systems in favor of lateral, peer-to-peer communications, and the depth of this division is bitterly played out in what we call "social media" every day.

There is no sense of community anymore—no "one nation, under God, indivisible"—and we are a people bickering and at each other's throats. The press no longer functions with the public trust, for journalists have been exposed as biased, manipulative, and in it for themselves. Spiro Agnew's famous speech about the power of television news—while thoroughly dismissed by the press at the time—turns out to have been prescient:

> ...the president of the United States has a right to communicate directly with the people who elected him, and the people of this country have the right to make up their own minds and form their own opinions about a presidential address, without having the president's words and thoughts characterized through the prejudice of hostile critics before they can even be digested.[1]

At CBN in the early 1980s, we hammered home the idea of a liberal bias in the press, which has turned out to be a lasting cultural contribution, as the success of Fox News demonstrates. The press has yet to fully accept this idea, however, even though the artificial hegemony of "objectivity" has today been replaced by the concept of transparency.

The American ideal of oneness through assimilated diversity—the dream of which Martin Luther King once spoke—has been crushed under the weight of well-intentioned groups who prefer the country as a tapestry of many different types of people rather than as a melting pot with unified ideals.

In the midst of this today, a master manipulator, showman, and salesman has seized power in Washington by exploiting fear, repeating themes that resonate with certain Americans, and promising simple solutions to complex problems facing the country. Intellectuals, media, and political observers are still puzzled by how Donald Trump was elected President and are positing theory upon theory as to why his followers heeded his call.

The reality, however, is that they were never heeding his call; he heeded and responded to their call. Donald Trump is skilled at deciphering the voice of those who feel disenfranchised by the culture and where it's heading. As a salesman, Mr. Trump sensed an entry point into the minds of his sales targets, initiating his innate ability, which then enabled him to articulate a product that sold. All he had to do was to paint a black and white, dystopian view of America and offer himself as the solution. This is not original thinking, for all he was doing was repeating the things discussed in the back rooms of white evangelicals, and we at CBN were the ones who planted many of those thoughts. These people are many of the same ones we organized and nurtured thirty years ago with *The 700 Club*, and I feel responsible, at least in part. As executive producer of the program during the season up to and including Pat Robertson's run for president in 1988, I helmed every part of what we put on TV, the result of which was a very deliberate and profound turning of the Republican Party to the right.

We knew exactly what we were doing, too. Armed with research at every step, we presented a form of Christianity that included getting involved in politics at every level. God wanted us to wrest control away from those who were destroying the Christian foundation of the country, and Virginia Beach was the most appropriate location from which to do it. It was here, after all, where English settlers first landed in the new world and planted a cross on the beach, dedicating the land to "our Lord and savior, Jesus Christ." There is a monument to this 1607 event at the northern end of Virginia Beach, where the settlers originally set foot on the continent. That gave us all the authority we felt we needed to finish the work that had begun there almost four centuries earlier.

Everything we presented was done with a sense of urgency due to what we felt was the pending return of Jesus Christ as prophesied in the Book of Revelation. Israel was the key to our understanding, for certain Christian teachings state that Jesus won't return until God has given Jerusalem back to Israel, which had begun in 1948 when Zionists—through an executive order from the United Nations following World War II and the subsequent "war" against Arabs who disagreed—began to seize land, water, and structures from Arabs who had lived in the Holy Land for millennia. Now that Jerusalem was back on a map labeled "Israel," we taught that the return of Jesus was imminent, and that meant we had to prepare. We claimed the role of John the Baptist in "preparing the way of the Lord," which gave us license to say and do whatever we felt was necessary in establishing God's kingdom on earth.

This belief was furthered by the words of many others and in books like 1970's *The Late Great Planet Earth* and later in the *Left Behind* series of novels, which reference the re-establishment of Israel. We taught a literal interpretation of Jesus' proclamation that, in the end, He will remember those who support Israel and cast aside those who do not. It was simply the right thing to do in the wake of such strong, albeit convenient, evidence that a movement of God was underway in the United States.

We certainly weren't alone in this task. Billy Graham had been telling the story of salvation for decades and was the friend of presidents from Harry Truman to Barack Obama. Jerry Falwell and his Moral Majority grassroots political movement was certainly also vocal. However, CBN had at least two unique aspects to the ministry that would put us at the forefront of change. One was Pat Robertson, his pedigree, his knowledge, and his insightful and brilliant political mind. Two, we fronted for Charismatic Christianity, which was a key part of the revival of the late 1970s and early 1980s. This gave us advantages over other Christian leaders and ministries and made our work singular in shifting Republican Party emphasis to the right. And a key component of both was a special classification in the world for the state of Israel.

And if the Jews of Israel were our friends, then the Muslims of the Arab world had to be the enemy, for there were no shades of grey in the worldview we presented. At home, we struck a chord with Christians over issues deemed an attack on the basic structure of the traditional family. In doing so, we were convinced that

God was on our side, for nothing in our manual could justify the murder of innocent unborn babies, the normalization of homosexuality, the de-sanctification of marriage between a man and a woman, public schools teaching contrary to the faith including the removal of the Ten Commandments and restrictions on prayer, the theft of our resources by the government, and the relentless pursuit by liberals to take what was ours and give it to others. When everything was taken into consideration, this was a powerful message to people in the trenches of America, the same people Donald Trump exploited in winning the election for president.

Before there was Fox News, there was *The 700 Club*, where everything was calculated to form a doable action plan for people who were predisposed to anger over the direction in which the country was headed. Again, we were heroes swooping in to rescue America from the influences of the devil. Or so we thought. And we were quite serious.

It would be foolish and naïve, however, to portray this fully as a religious movement, for to do so would dismiss very similar strategies and tactics we saw during the candidacy of Donald Trump. We were the ones, after all, who led the movement of politics to the right, the result of which we have with us today. Christian or otherwise, the Republican Party is now so far to the right that it's beginning to resemble historical fascism, with Mr. Trump's increasingly radical proclamations about somehow removing Muslims and others he deems undesirable from our midst.

In June 2016, Orlando, Florida was the scene of a gay nightclub rampage by a lapsed Muslim, Omar Mateen, with an AR-15-type assault rifle and severe psychological issues regarding homosexuals.

Nearly fifty people were killed and another fifty wounded when Mateen opened fire inside the club. He had just earlier jumped aboard the ISIS train, so the terrorist group claimed responsibility, which dominated early press coverage.

Predisposed to a worldview that includes Islam as the enemy, Mr. Trump bragged that he was the only candidate telling "the truth" about Muslim immigrants. Mateen, however, turned out to be a US citizen, not an immigrant, but that didn't matter to Mr. Trump. Pat Robertson went on the air the day after the massacre and condemned both the perpetrator and the gay victims, saying that Christians should just wait on the sidelines and let the homosexuals and the Muslims kill each other. Pat, it would seem, has become even more extreme than he was when I was his producer.

The point is that both Donald Trump and Pat Robertson address the same people, those who practice a form of Christianity so foreign to orthodoxy that it truly boggles the intelligence. We stood high atop our satellite-based pedestal in the 1980s and shouted down to a citizenry whose minds were fertile for a different perspective. We fed them. We nurtured them. How we did it and got away with it holds a key to unraveling the frustrating reality we have before us today.

Jesus is now clearly linked with Republican Party politics. He has joined the GOP, and *The 700 Club* is the principal tool that put Him there. Whether He wishes to be there is irrelevant in today's political arena, as is whether God in the form of Jesus Christ wants to be associated with Republican Party social positions as righteous. Perception is reality, and even if one can make the case that the heart of Jesus might be closer to the Democrats, that's not how it's being played out today.

This is a book for Christians of all stripes, because Christians are the only ones who can make this right. The angry mob of the early twenty-first century won't listen to anybody else—certainly not outsiders—for they've been taught that everybody else is in it for unrighteous reasons. This is the sad state in which we find ourselves today.

The thousands or perhaps millions of Christians influenced by *The 700 Club* over the last four decades are good people. Their intentions are noble. They mostly wish that others would find the peace and contentment they've discovered for themselves. Along the way, however, the essential gospel call about feeding sheep and lambs has been overshadowed by a perceived need to not just challenge the evolution of our culture but also directly participate in what they view as its restoration. Certain Christian leaders whose motives—while presented as above reproach—have fed them Biblical mandates that seem to justify this participation. However, a deeper examination reveals that the gospel being most preached today is a form of self-centeredness: the gospel of self.

I know this, because I helped teach it while serving as Pat Robertson's producer and executive producer during a most critical point in the TV program's development, the 1980s, when Pat himself decided that God had called him to run for president and that he would win. The story of how this happened is my story, and the gospel of self is the dark side of that chronicle.

History will record that *The 700 Club* was the taproot of that which moved the Republican Party to the right and provided the political support today for a man like Donald Trump. A 2015 Harvard report concluded that right-wing media was driving the GOP,[2] not Republican leadership, but this assumes that in order for people to behave as cultural radicals, they must be manipulated into doing so. This is a misleading interpretation of human nature and the power of personal faith. It would be absurd to suggest that the many elements of right-wing media didn't play a role in this, but those who challenge this right turn by the GOP need to look far beyond the institutional power of media to influence. Conservative talk radio, Fox News, offline publications, and the hundreds of online observer websites would simply not exist without an audience driven by a faith-mandated conscience and thusly predisposed to their messages. We knew this at CBN in the early 1980s, and as long as we could present current events in what we called "a Biblical perspective," people would take an interest.

This is the gap in understanding that blinds the mainstream press in their attempts to understand the "success" of right-wing media, especially Fox News. Because the press regards religion and the viewpoints of the religious as within what's known in journalism as the Sphere of Deviance,[3] it will never see itself as anything other than balanced. People of faith do not agree with the view of being placed on the outside of culture's norm, and that's why the Fox slogan "Fair and Balanced" works so well.

This form of Christianity blends so well with the Republican Party because both are formed around a circle with self at the center. This was the overarching albeit unwritten strategy of Pat Robertson, although there were many in key positions at CBN who either weren't aware of this or simply refused to see it. To me, it was pretty obvious and was later proven in a memorable private discussion I had with Pat about fundraising.

The 700 Club began as a Christian talk show for the faithful, but its evolution into a politically motivated, point-of-view news program began in bits and pieces before I arrived and accelerated afterwards. In an address to a noon prayer meeting in April of 1981, Pat Robertson offered the vision he wanted to fulfill and the Biblical justification for moving the ministry in that direction:

> And I tell you, in our world today; people are like a bunch of sheep. They're saying, 'What must we do? You know, what do we do with our money? What do we do with our children? What do we do with our education? What do we vote for?' And all these—What do we do? And somehow or other God's got to give some people with knowledge of the times to tell Israel what they ought to do. And I think we have a golden opportunity to do that, and that's one of the things we're trying to do on *The 700 Club*.

That was Pat in 1981.

So the vision was set and the only missing element was money. After all, CBN was a ministry. It paid no taxes as a media company, and the tax exemption was worth far more than any for-profit business model, especially in 1981. Pat Robertson was a brilliant marketer, however, and despite his professed faith in God to take care of providing resources, very little at CBN was left to chance, and that applied especially to fund-raising. Only a small part of marketing is creative or innovative; most of the blue-collar efforts involved processes and were extremely scientific.

We knew, for example, what percentage of 700 Club Members—at fifteen dollars a month—would covert to 1000 Club Members—at eighty-three dollars a month—and we knew, on average, how long that conversion would take. We had the same data in terms of converting 1000 Club Members to 2500 Club Members, and turning those members into Founders Club members. Based on past growth, this allowed us to extrapolate a budget projection, and that's what we used to make our plans.

But behind it all was the mind of a fundraising genius, a man who understood human nature like few others, and mostly a man who was unafraid to exploit that understanding in a justified means to what he felt was a righteous end. I learned how to raise money directly from Pat Robertson, and his methodology might surprise the faithful, for it is built on self-centeredness. And if the core of its ability to raise money is built on selfishness, then it must follow that the CBN message itself must do likewise. This is the secret truth behind what we intended to present as a movement of God's spirit on the earth.

In February 1985, as I was gaining more authority at the ministry of *The 700 Club*, I asked Pat if he would teach me everything he knew about raising money. We went to lunch, and I took copious notes. Here's what he told me, according to my notes:

> We don't necessarily have to present everything as a crisis, but it's impossible to make a change when everybody feels good about existing circumstances. That's the mistake

Reagan has made. He got re-elected but now faces difficulty in implementing change, since he sold the country on the fact that everything is hunky-dory.

It's basically like John the Baptist. The axe is laid to the root of the tree and people are saying, 'What shall we do?'

We need to tie the spiritual with the natural (meaning current events). He told the people what to do in light of the current events. We need to do the same thing, because if you can do that, you really have something that's worth something.

Here's what motivates people to give to CBN, and in this order:

It helps me.
It helps my family.
It helps my community.
It helps my nation.
I'm fulfilling the great commission, spreading the gospel to the world.
It's my duty.
I'll get blessed if I do.
I'm helping others who are poorer than me.

It's like a finely tuned orchestra. You don't play all bass and you don't play all treble. Together, they make a wonderful sound.

People also like to be part of a winner. Nobody likes to lose.

Challenges are important, because people are goal-oriented and respond to peer pressure.

Bargains are important, like building a $13 million building for $100.

There is also a thing of the old folks wanting to help the young, sort of to perpetuate society somehow.

What Pat Robertson taught me that day was that success in Christian television ministry began with tweaking the self-centered core of human nature. Notice that he painted a picture of expanding circles, each moving away from the recognition of self at the center. Helping the poor is at the bottom of the list, almost as though that particular motivation is separate from the rest, and this was played out in our use of Operation Blessing to hit a particular kind of Christian giver. The rest, however, formed the core of our ministry and our fundraising.

Armed with this kind of direction, it was easy to craft not only fund-raising but also everything else associated with *The 700 Club* television program. Taking over the country for God wasn't so much positioned as a duty; it was more like "you need to do this for yourself and your family." It's a subtle difference in the marketing practice of positioning, but it's a much more powerful motivator. This is core Pat Robertson, and nothing he did, said, or accomplished makes sense without this layer of understanding included in the final analysis.

There was nothing sinister about it to us; it was a sincere and genuine desire to change the world for good, although its ultimate fruit has been chaotic, divisive, and dangerous. We felt the hand

of God guided us, and I write that in all sincerity. We looked at
progressive culture and saw only evil. We felt animosity against
Christianity and the church. We were mocked and ridiculed in the
media, especially that which was coming from Hollywood. We felt
that God was giving things over to us to make things right. What
we didn't see was the trap of our motives being driven by self. After
all, does God really need us to fix things that we viewed as wrong?

Even Pat's acclaimed manual for living, *The Secret Kingdom*, is a
diagram for using the Bible to justify a lifestyle that is built around
self, self-gain, and self-betterment based on the above expanding
circle. It's a self-help book disguised as theology. Every "law"
proclaimed is designed to help individual people, families, and
communities get ahead in the realm of human competition. You
can make yourself healthier, wealthier, safer, happier, and more
dominant in the culture simply by living within these "laws of
the Kingdom." It's a beautiful companion to the teaching I was
given about fundraising and further evidence that we were really
teaching a very insidious form of selfishness, the gospel of self.

This, again, is why we all must look to the mirror in order to
solve society's problems. Pogo got it right when he said, "I have seen
the enemy, and he is us." The church desperately needs a season of
self-examination and the courage to stand up and say, "Enough!"
The hope for this is virtually nil, however, as long we point our fin-
gers at others and say that the problem is theirs and not ours.

And so we use Facebook and other forms of social media today
to pass along false memes that fit our worldview. We express our
condescending disgust about the behaviors of others as if somehow
it will rub off on us if we don't. Our radar is what matters, not

truth. We hear or see some piece of media that pings the familiar circulating screen that stands guard over us, and we feel it necessary to pass it along for validation by those we hope to influence. Why? Because it helps me, it helps my family, it helps my community, it helps my nation, it's my duty, and I'll get blessed if I do.

Even the Great Commission of Matthew 24 has been tilted so as to become a measuring stick of sorts for the health of a church, a preacher, or an evangelist. If not, why do churches and evangelists count salvations? What does it matter, if the motive is truly love? It's that little pat on the back that we all seek, evidence of our righteousness and a hedge against eternity in hell. This is, of course, self-driven, self-motivated, and self-centered. It's not the deed that matters; it's the recognition thereof. Don't get me wrong; I know plenty of people who have a real heart for people they deem "lost," but it's very difficult for any of us, as human beings, to avoid the trap of self in well-doing. We just want so badly to do well (and be recognized for it).

The second time I went through the twelve steps of Alcoholics Anonymous many years ago, I met each Saturday morning with my sponsor Steve. We both attended a wonderful Saturday morning group and met for breakfast beforehand to discuss my progress with the steps. I badly wanted and needed to please him, for he was a key part of the process of living a sober life. One Saturday morning, Steve gave me an assignment. "During the coming week," he said, "I want you to give up one hour of your time to help other people." He went on to give me the rules. "You can do one thing for an hour, or many things that add up to an hour, like giving up a really good parking place for somebody else."

"You can't tell anybody about any of this," he continued, "but make yourself a list to keep track of what you've accomplished. Bring that list with you next week."

I was excited and did exactly what was required. I chose to keep track of little things I had done and brought my list with me the following Saturday morning.

"Did you bring your list?" Steve inquired. Beaming, I pulled it from my pocket and started to open it to share it with him.

"Wait a minute," he stopped me cold. "You can't show that to me, right? The deal was you couldn't tell anybody what you did."

I was stunned. I wanted so badly to show him how well I had done the assignment, but he was more interested in teaching me about the insidious nature of self-centeredness. It called into question my motive, and isn't this something with which we all struggle? We want to be rewarded in any way possible, and isn't this why some posts on Facebook are from those seeking a pat on the back for something nice they did or how they blessed somebody else? This is the tricky part of human nature, and its presence in addicts is over-the-top.

But we all must deal with it as we walk through life, especially those on the road less travelled. It's why the gospel of self is so easy to sell and why the consequences of its deception are so devastating and hard to overcome. We can be so caught up in the desire to serve a loving God and be a good person—something we view as contrary to "the world"—that we find comfort with anyone expressing a similar motivation. Consequently, we miss the self-centered social engineering that's actually taking place and, in the process, confuse bad behavior with good intentions.

Selfishness and self-centeredness form the most dangerous epidemic facing Western Civilization today. And what is extreme selfishness but intolerance itself? On the highway, I'm more important than you are, so get out of my way, and don't even think that I'll get out of yours. In fact, you don't have the rights I have behind the wheel, so why not just get off the road entirely? Why should I have to tolerate anybody else, when I'm the most important person on the highway anyway?

This kind of thinking is evident everywhere, though its most common proponents usually wouldn't think of themselves as such, and it breeds intolerance, especially in religion and politics. Why should I have to tolerate you, the thinking goes, if I'm right? My religion, my political party, my opinion is what's right and best, so everybody just get out of the way and let me run things. The mind of the ideologue is totalitarian, and nothing gives purity to such deception like the zeal of religion, especially if the perception of absolute authority governs that religion. It's not really my opinion then; I'm speaking for God!

This is an incredibly destructive force, and it poisons people, families, whole communities and even nations. It's doubly corrosive, because it hides an unspoken fear that my covenant with God is somehow tied to my ability to help others with my love. And if I don't?

We exploited everything possible in the spreading of our message, including the powerful motivator of envy. Testimony stories about healings or fiscal prosperity always led to the proclamation that "this is available for you." As you'll read later, we very rarely spoke about those who didn't get "blessed," for the carrot on the stick was believed to be an important element of building people's faith. But faith in what? That's the dark side of the telling of my story, and it causes me physical pain today, as I witness the deep split in our culture. The people doing the dividing aren't aware that they've been duped, so this book is a cleansing, of sorts, for me—my amends for the role that I played in this. Please. I'm sorry.

As the Republican Party drifts farther to the right, Evangelical Christians find themselves in the position of having to deny that they've become exactly what they despise—a group of elites trying to force their beliefs on others. Within this denial, the twisting of truth is self-serving. Democrats are demonized as socialists, communists, Marxists, and of course, liberals who want to steal from them in the name of government control of their lives. The obvious conflict here is the idea that God is somehow unable to deal with this absent their help.

Maybe America is under judgment right now. Maybe God is sick and tired of all our shenanigans, including those being done in His name. Maybe our cultural problems are all a reflection of the gospel of self, and God is judging not the world but the church. I'm reminded of the story of Jesus being brought before Pontius Pilate for the crime of being declared "King of the Jews." His response was that He was "not of this world" and if He were, His followers would fight to free Him. We are unable to see ourselves in this position, for it seems we are fighting to save the wrong world.

And through the Republican Party of all things. After all, it helps me, it helps my family, it helps my community, it helps my nation, it's my duty, and I'll get blessed if I do.

Two

The Commission and the Mission

To argue with a person who has renounced the use of reason is like administering medicine to the dead.

—Thomas Paine

I had a rather miraculous born-again experience while working as host and producer of *PM Magazine* in Louisville, Kentucky in 1980. It happened as I was driving my car from a meeting with an Evangelical Christian in his A-frame house in the forests of Southern Indiana. We had been discussing my life of depression, sex, suicide, drugs, and alcohol, while he talked to me about his faith. I cried non-stop the entire trip and fell asleep exhausted when I got home.

The next morning, it seemed like everything had changed for me. I felt wonderful, my depression had lifted, I no longer felt the need for drugs, and the most amazing thing was that my language had been completely transformed, as I simply could not curse. I ceremoniously dumped all of my drugs and paraphernalia into the Ohio River and went about my life as a different person.

At work, I put up a poster of a Monarch butterfly with the words "Born Again." I got involved with a small family ministry in Southern Indiana and wrote scores of songs for the contemporary Christian band Revival. I was energized and felt alive like I hadn't ever felt before. I felt a sense of purpose, one of glorifying God and the creation. I wanted to sing, and I couldn't stop smiling. I was a desperate, despondent, and dying drug abuser on a path to destruction, and overnight, I was the opposite. I felt at peace with my religious roots and fully in love with the character of Jesus. That fullness of love made me feel amazing. I felt clean. I wanted to give. I wanted to put something into the world. I wanted to be a help and a blessing to others. Mostly, I wanted to tell everybody about what had happened to me.

I also started watching Christian television, for I wanted to learn everything I could. This included programs like *The 700 Club* and teaching programs featuring intelligent people—or at least those who seemed intelligent—like Kenneth Copeland, Charles Stanley, and James Robison.

I got a letter one day from a student at what was then CBN University. She was doing her thesis on "magazine show burnout," a phenomenon that negatively impacts people who did what I was doing. She told me she was surveying producers of *PM Magazine* about the topic and asked that I fill out her survey form and send it back. I did and received a phone call from her the next week. She told me that my answers were different than most, and she said I "must be a Christian." I told her yes, and she asked if I had ever considered working for CBN. She asked that I send her a tape of my work and that she would pass it along to the ministry. I complied.

The first story on my tape was a six-minute piece about a horse photographer from Lexington, the home of thoroughbred racing. It featured Secretariat, the famous Triple Crown winner, and how this photographer worked with horses to get perfect composition photos. One section revealed his secret for getting the horse's attention, so that its ears would point perfectly forward. He played an audiotape of a mare in heat walking through a barn of stallions.

Pat Robertson's second love was thoroughbred horses, and I was told he was fascinated by this story. I was invited to Virginia Beach to interview for a job with *The 700 Club*. I went and met Executive Producer Michael Little and the rest of the CBN heavyweights. They were particularly intrigued by the relatively small amount of time it took me to produce the horse story, for the role of story producer was much different with *PM Magazine* than it apparently was for them. It was a heady trip, because they offered me a job, but I had misgivings and turned them down. I felt comfortable doing what I was doing, and the truth is I really wasn't ready to work for a large Christian ministry. I was still a baby in the faith.

For all its glory, being on TV isn't for everybody. Oh, it was heady having my picture on the side of every bus in town, but I hated being recognized everywhere in Louisville. I had to always be "on" in public, because viewers of the show would recognize me. My wife took great joy in playfully embarrassing me wherever, and I began to regret the job. The loss of privacy was a weight that I couldn't bear, so I made a career shift and became a field producer for the second magazine show that the station aired, *Louisville Tonight*. I learned more in that year about storytelling than I'd learned in two previous jobs doing the work, for the team that produced the show was made up of national video photographer award winners. I honed my craft and continued working with the music ministry of Revival. I grew in many, many ways in that year and truly became a high-end television producer.

I had also become a deeply serious student of the Bible and all things pertaining to the faith. I poured through book after book in a search for meaning and understanding about the things of the spirit. My files are filled with journal entries about what I was learning, as the "one-potato, two-potato, three-potato, four" march to wisdom continued. I watched Christian television, but mostly I watched as the culture seemed to slip away from what I had known during my childhood. As a professional observer of life, the stirring in my soul to explore these events was unmistakable. I wanted to know the whys of everything, especially why people behaved the way they did. As a child, my faith was all about simple acceptance and basic values of hard work, discipline, and persistence, but life had shown me that questions were important, too. I wanted answers to everything, and I felt my mind was fertile ground for new and exciting ideas, whereas it had only before known grounded tradition. I wanted to fly.

The economy was collapsing everywhere in early 1981, and soon the management of *Louisville Tonight* had to make difficult business decisions. Because I had come from *PM Magazine*, my salary was higher than any other producer on the staff of *Louisville Tonight*, so my job was eliminated in the budget squeeze.

The first call I made was to CBN, where news of my unemployment was greeted with suggestions that this was God moving in my life and calling me to the ministry. "The hound of heaven" is what they called it. I couldn't (or didn't want to) argue with that, and so we moved to Virginia Beach where I became the manager of the field crews who proudly produced the stories for *The 700 Club*.

I knew magazine show production processes and systems like no one else at CBN. The university had a marvelous film school, and it cranked out wonderful producers. But daily magazine shows are a different animal, one with a voracious appetite for content. It demands discipline at every turn using electronic news gathering (ENG) equipment, systems, and training, and I knew how to teach this to the ministry. I created an algebraic formula to prove to Pat Robertson that the program was vastly understaffed. He wanted two fresh testimony stories for every program, and that required an upgrade. We hired more people, and soon I was made producer and then senior producer of the program itself.

As producer, the first thing I did was to bring state-of-the-arts graphics production into the program. I hired the top guy in the TV industry, Ben Blank from ABC-TV, to consult with us, and our goal was to outdo Ted Turner in what he was accomplishing at CNN by moving graphics production away from engineers and into the hands of artists. More than anything else, this dramatically boosted the production quality of *The 700 Club*.

Regardless of what people may think about the content we presented back then, even the most cynical of television critics would have to admit that the production values of the program were outstanding, and I am most proud of that. It was, however, the mission of the ministry that drove me; making a difference was my personal motivation for making television in the first place, whether it was in the news business or what we did at CBN.

The missions of *The 700 Club* and CBN were compelling, interesting, and very doable using the reach of television.

The 700 Club

The mission of *The 700 Club* is to provide a television vehicle to accomplish the Mission of The Christian Broadcasting Network. In doing so it serves as the principal platform for corporate development activities.

Strategy

Through the use of preproduced material, interviews, and graphics, we will present a Biblical perspective of news and current events.

In all that we do, we will present the Gospel of Jesus Christ in relevant, modern terms.

There exists in America a very negative attitude about Christians and Christianity. This is especially true among skeptics and interferes with our message. Therefore, we will, whenever possible, try to present a youthful, joyful image of Christianity.

We believe revival is accomplished "Not by strength, not by might, not by power, but by my spirit saith the Lord." Since the miraculous always accompanies genuine outpouring of the Holy Spirit, and He has promised to "confirm His Word with signs and wonders," we are absolutely committed to documenting and revealing the miraculous wherever possible.

We will lift up Jesus in all that we say and do.

We will follow the Apostle Paul's example to "be all things to all men that by all means we might save some" in our effort to reach a dying world. We will also follow our Lord's example and "eat with publicans and sinners." In doing so, it is understood that we may, from time to time, face the wrath of the Pharisees in defending program content they either disagree with or do not understand.

Through regular, promotable series reports we will present information unavailable elsewhere on television.

Our program will entertain, educate, and enlighten.

All of our segments will be presented in such a way that each offers a Biblical answer to the conflict presented.

Wherever possible, we will build bridges over denominational walls as we seek unity in accordance with the Laws of the Kingdom of God.

In preproduced pieces, through the spoken word, and with graphics we will present the Laws of God's Kingdom. Our goal is that all would learn in practical terms what it means to live the Christian lifestyle and that all would mature in Christ.

We will coordinate with corporate development to assure the smooth, on-going flow of spots, features, guests, and graphics, which illustrate the activities of all of the branches of the CBN ministry.

Few television programs have their own mission statements, and the above gave me a general outline from which to proceed every day. It was also very useful for me in "managing upward" with the executive staff of the ministry, those who were charged with bottom line maintenance and with whom I often had conflicts in running the operation. Key to the mission statement were sections about current events, miracles, and teaching the "Laws of God's Kingdom," for these were the hallmarks of *The 700 Club* and essential to producing the program.

The program's mission statement wasn't the document that got the most attention, however. The overarching mission of the ministry was what guided everything we did, and this document was shared both internally and publicly. It is here where we bent our own rules in seeking political change in the land, for laws that restrict tax-exempt organizations govern such activities.

The Christian Broadcasting Network

The mission of CBN and its affiliated organizations is to prepare the United States of America, the nations of the Middle East, the Far East, South America, and other selected nations of the world for the coming of Jesus Christ and the establishment of the Kingdom of God on earth. Our ultimate goal is to achieve a time in history when "the knowledge of the Lord will cover the earth as the waters cover the sea."

In achieving our mission our chief method is the strategic use of mass communication, especially radio, television, and film; the distribution of records, cassettes, films and literature; and the conduct of education that will train the young and old to understand how the principles of the Kingdom of God relate to those spheres of human endeavor which play a dominant role in our world.

In achieving our mission nothing should be done that does not glorify God and His Son Jesus Christ.

Three words should characterize the execution of our mission. First, we will be innovative. Our task is not to duplicate or copy other men's labors. Second, we will be excellent. Our work must either be of lasting value and highest quality or it should not be done at all. Third, we will demonstrate integrity. In our work, our public relations, our internal and external communications, there will be an abiding commitment to truth. Integrity must characterize all of our dealings with others.

In staffing for our mission we must insist on securing the best possible men and women for each task, and we will make every effort to see that people and tasks are matched appropriately. Our policy will be to secure a small staff of outstanding people and to compensate them well for their labors. Our staff should be "filled with the Holy Spirit and wisdom." God's work must be done by God's people, equipped and chosen.

Implicit in the fulfillment of our mission is the demonstration of all of the principles of the Kingdom of God, especially that of reciprocity. Therefore, we continually endeavor to give generous assistance to the relief of human need and suffering through the world as well as donations to other organizations that share our basic objectives.

We believe that God's work, done according to the principles of His Kingdom, will prosper financially. We cannot serve God and money, so service to God and his Call always takes precedence over conflicting considerations of money. Nevertheless, we recognize that only those activities which are economically viable can continue in our present society, so planning must take into account economic viability. We also categorically state that the payment of accounts when due is a key ingredient of integrity. We seek to finance our activities by all lawful and morally correct means, including but not limited to contributions, sales, and investment income. In planning we will endeavor to project adequate income for current activities, plus generous surpluses from which we can build and expand.

In the fulfillment of our mission, as to calling and message, our Biblical role model is John the Baptist. As to wisdom it is Solomon. As to ministry to Israel it is the prophet Ezekiel. In all that we are, do, and say it is Jesus Christ.

This was the governing document of CBN, but it was stretched in every direction in attempts to accomplish the task of bringing the "knowledge of the Lord" to America. The fine line between preaching and government influence was breached time and again and included such activities as funding political action with ministry monies. Excellence, innovation, and integrity: I heard those words constantly, and it's hard to argue that we didn't operate regularly with the first two. When it came to integrity, however, we let our political ambitions overrun our commitment to this important value.

My role was chief architect of the mission statement, and I served that role well. It was this, however, that put me at odds with several key executives, those who were more interested in managing the words of the mission than the actual task of implementing it.

This is why I often felt very alone in my job, for I was unafraid of chaos and willing to lead a course through its stormy seas. This is also why I enjoyed a special bond with Pat Robertson, for I could anticipate him better than most, and this is the mark of a good producer. In my life as a TV talent, I had once been made to look like a fool during a live broadcast because the producer hadn't timed the program correctly. I swore after that event that if I ever got into producing, I would never allow somebody on the air to falter due to my inability to anticipate trouble or time a show correctly.

We created what was lovingly referred to as a "living format" for live television. It was the only thing that could accommodate Pat's continuously editing mind, for he often went with his gut in calling for adjustments to the show. As I look back, it was really quite remarkable that we could create flawless television production as it was being adjusted from the anchor chair.

I could "see" Pat's mind work in real time and gave him options on where to take a thought stream as he was thinking it. Many was the time that I would hand him something off camera while he was talking live that would naturally flow into, for example, fund-raising or political action. This was my job, not simply the making of television, and I did it well, regardless of how it influenced relations with others in the ministry.

As far as I was concerned, my duty was to Pat Robertson, not any of his appointed executive representatives. There were many, many conflicts in this arena, but I stood firm in my convictions. After all, a ministry is not like a business corporation, where power and control flow down a hierarchical pyramid. A ministry more closely resembles a cult of personality, where the person with the "calling" is the sole authority, and everyone else is assembled to bring that about. I viewed my own personal calling as helping Pat Robertson do just that.

As such, I played a key role in the nurturing of our audience on the principles that the mission statement acknowledged, but this included stretching things as far as they would go. For example, it says nothing about politics in the mission statement, and yet, as the son of a US Senator, Pat Robertson was a political animal, perhaps even ahead of his calling to the ministry. He understood politics like few others, for the political process was often to blame for societal miseries that he was convinced God wanted to correct. Pat knew the players and how the games were played. His observations were regularly spot-on, and he knew what he was doing whenever he opened his mouth with a political perspective on any issue.

For example, Pat told Ben Kinchlow and Danuta Soderman during one off-the-cuff, unscripted conversation on the air live that only Christians and Jews were qualified to hold public office in the United States. Ben expressed shock, but Pat repeated what he had just said. Many people—including NBC News—pointed to this moment as evidence that Pat was far outside what journalist Daniel C. Hallin calls the "sphere of legitimate debate,"[4] but Pat was speaking directly to his constituency and didn't care how his critics would interpret it. To those who believe the US was built upon Judeo-Christian principles, it's easy to accept a statement that only Jews and Christians would be qualified to run it, but this concept is foreign to those who believe the Founding Fathers were more inclusive and tolerant. More often than not, this was the case with statements that might seem outrageous to others, especially liberals, and was why we felt we needed to educate them.

That does not mean he was always right in his addressing of the issues. I recall one day when the Supreme Court made a ruling involving school prayer after we had finished the live, 10:00 a.m. program. Pat called the team together later in the day, so that we could record a new version of the opening news segment that would address the matter. He was angry over what he viewed as yet another stab by liberal thinkers into the heart of "Christian" America.

The news department hastily put together a piece about the ruling, and we gathered in the studio to record the new opening segment. Everyone was in the same clothes they wore for the morning broadcast, so that the final show would be seamless. After the story and discussion, Pat asked that everyone—including the audience—pray with him about the matter. I remember standing there with CBN President Bob Slosser, as Pat prayed that God remove those Supreme Court justices who voted against prayer by any means necessary, including their deaths. Bob and I looked at each other and said almost simultaneously, "He can't say that on television!" We both knew that Pat was very angry over the court's decision, but to actually call for the deaths of justices who had voted for the ban was both unwise and dangerous, to say nothing of the immorality of such a public statement.

We asked everyone to hold their positions and gave Pat our concerns. After much consideration, he agreed to record another version without the death threats, and that was the one we used. This was a rare opportunity for a mulligan in his often highly edgy proclamations about government, patriotism, and duty that were a regular part of *The 700 Club*. It's hard to say if Pat actually calculated or even considered his words before making statements like killing Supreme Court justices. He was very smart, and he knew his audience well, but he was also very much a believer in the power of prayer to provide answers for individual believers and groups. Given the breadth and depth of our mission, Pat envisioned himself in the driver's seat of a great vehicle that God Himself had provided for the purpose of moving America away from its liberal drift. I think he was sincere in so doing, and those who see his actions only as the aspirations of greed, power, or personal gain are the same people struggling today to understand the election of Donald Trump.

As the months and years went by and the Reagan presidency was beginning to wind down, *The 700 Club* became more and more political. In retrospect, we were preaching that having faith in God to change people's hearts and in that way change culture wasn't enough, and that He wanted us all to get involved in politics. It was a subtle shift, but we weren't alone. The entire televangelist world was slipping away from its first love and drifting into the traps of power and influence. As *The 700 Club* evolved, we were educating people that the Republican way was God's way, and that went on to become one of the most remarkable feats of social engineering of the twentieth century.

Pat Robertson loves maps, and he was right in his belief that a great many people have no idea where this country or that one is located, much less how they interact with their neighbors. They certainly didn't know why that was important or how matters "over there" impacted those of us here. We created eight-foot panels with beautiful maps representing regions of the world.

I remember one day in the dressing room, Pat asked that we have the map of Africa available, because he wanted to talk about it. This wasn't a planned segment, so we all had to be on our toes. In about fifteen minutes, he went through every country on the continent, named the capital, the ruler, their politics, and explained the geo-political position vis-à-vis each country and how they related to their neighbors. I stood there and watched this, and I remember commenting to myself that there are only a very small handful of people in the entire world who could do what he had just done. It was truly a remarkable display of intellect, knowledge, and communications skill. His motivation was to teach, but as to mission, he needed to prove to his followers that CBN was a group of Biblical "men with knowledge of the times to guide Israel."

Pat didn't like liberals and thought they were a curse on society because they placed dependence on government ahead of dependence on God. Pat was also a strong proponent of personal responsibility and rejected any thoughts that people needed others to take care of them. Democrats were liberals, so Democrats were easily thought of as deceived enemies of God. And since we felt that the media was naturally biased toward liberalism due to background, education, and the lack of religious credentials, real or imagined, Pat wanted to present a conservative view that was based in the principles of God. Hence, we demonstrated an ongoing love affair with the GOP, and our slogan was "TV Journalism With A Different Spirit."

Everything about *The 700 Club* was carefully researched and strategized. We had as our guide the work of Pat's great friend George Gallup, and his studies of religion in America. We knew how evangelicals were perceived, and a key component of our strategy was to counter those views. Most people thought of evangelicals as ignorant, overweight, polyester-wearing, Bible-thumping morons for whom church going was a cover for hypocritical behavior. We showed the opposite on the program, even going so far as to avoid testimony stories featuring those who were overweight. We wanted stories of smart, young people, who would give the appearance to our viewers that evangelicalism was a good thing for them and their families. They could love God, have a strong family, be prosperous, feel a sense of "rightness," be respected leaders in their communities and make a difference. We needed to recruit people outside the bias demonstrated by Gallup, and that meant "coloring" our program to reflect different kinds of people while avoiding those who fit the stereotypes.

But there's a funny thing about stereotypes. There can often be truth at their core, and that was something none of us wanted to consider. We were, in fact, largely talking to ignorant, polyester-wearing, Bible-thumping morons, and they didn't possess the wherewithal to do anything but parrot and follow. This is a big part of the problem today, for I've encountered literally thousands of people we once targeted who have now gone off and are seeking different paths for themselves. What began as the dream of building a political army of intelligent, thinking people for the GOP has produced the opposite, and there are still many people functioning as though that's not the case.

Many of the intelligent, upscale, young, and attractive people we recruited abandoned the ministry—*all* TV ministries—in the wake of the televangelist scandals that were to come. This left few except the stereotypes, and this is something that doesn't get much attention from those who examine the era today.

I do not mean to suggest that everything we did was evil. God forbid! Helping people overcome difficulties is a noble, worthwhile, and righteous cause. We spread the love of God in ways that many were able to embrace, whether they stayed with us or not. We planted seeds and nurtured them. We "taught people to fish" as the old adage says. We taught people how to make a difference for themselves, their families, their communities, and beyond.

We gave people perspective about world events, and this was no small thing. We were up front about our bias and challenged others in media to be so as well. Transparency in subjective journalism was, in some ways, birthed at *The 700 Club*, and I'm proud of that.

We spoke for the powerless in matters before the courts and influenced decisions with intelligent reasoning that didn't exist before we made it happen. We educated smart people in media, public policy, and the law, knowing that their influence would spread exponentially.

We ministered to suffering people and gave them hope. We pleaded the cause of the poor and the afflicted wherever we could, and opened doors for people who had difficulty opening them alone.

We also served others in times of natural disasters and other needs throughout the world. We influenced policy for the better. We influenced government at levels big and small. We made a difference for people, societies, and institutions.

We served as a hub where intelligent people could gather, discuss Christianity, and create original concepts about such heady thoughts as a common thread to anchor the tapestry that America has become. There are many wonderful, actually remarkable people who are part of the mission and work of CBN, its Regent University, and other affiliates. These people work tirelessly trying to make the world a better place based upon the fundamentals of the Christian faith. I salute them and their efforts.

But in the end, as Edward R. Murrow once said, "We can deny our heritage and our history, but we cannot escape responsibility for the result." For all the good we did, we cannot escape a legacy that includes the creation of an angry mob, one driven by selfishness, self-pity, fear, self-righteousness, and ignorance, all in the name of Jesus. After all, if the same authority figure preaching Jesus also spoke on behalf of the GOP, how could followers possibly be wrong? Such is the logic of those who don't or can't think for themselves, and it created a monster. We should have known better.

Three

Life at CBN

Unless you have bad times, you can't appreciate the good times.

—Joe Torre

While I truly believe that I contributed much to the furtherance of the missions of CBN and *The 700 Club*, I also learned more in those five years than during any other work season of my life. It was an advanced education, a degree in Life itself. I learned deep lessons about people, the failures of hierarchies, social engineering, fundraising science, ethics and morality as they relate to news, politics, quality television production, live television, evil, deception, the power of television, the church, religion, human nature, history, journalism, and the power of information to corrupt, also known as propaganda.

Before Fox News ever claimed to be "fair and balanced," there was CBN News. Moreover, the study of life deep within a major Christian ministry is unlike studying any other kind of organization, for Christian people are capable of expressing great love as they're stabbing you in the back or otherwise trying to get their way. People don't stop being human just because they proclaim Christianity, but Christian behavior is often quite the opposite. The idea that "the ground is level at the foot of the cross" introduces a fascinating form of insubordination into a business setting, but beyond that, it also makes for remarkable— and not always favorable—interaction between differing societal strata. One would think that the common bond of being in the same lifeboat would produce a sweet form of humility, but it more often did the opposite, and nowhere was this more evident than in our political views. Despite proclamations that our war was spiritual, we fought at the grassroots of culture to "win" for God at all levels.

Little did I realize at the time how this dramatically weakened my/our beliefs in the capabilities of an almighty God, for we were often quoted the words of the "Shakespeare of Divines," seventeenth century Anglican cleric Jeremy Taylor: "Whatever we beg of God, let us also work for it, if the thing be matter of duty, or a consequent to industry; for God loves to bless labour and reward it, but not to support idleness."[5] The problem here is that this is an intellectual concept that demands a degree of discernment in order to carry out. While Pat and others were certainly capable of that, I'm not sure this can apply to those who don't share such gifts. This includes the angry mob that functions as the Christian Right today.

In my experience with not only my own walk but also in working with hundreds of alcoholics, God works from the inside out, not the other way around and certainly not from the top down. Moreover, the choice of directing believers to the Republican Party is illogical and unreasonable. I can say without question that the ministry of Jesus was most definitely not one of "pick yourself up by your bootstraps and get to work!" God is both just *and* merciful, and it takes a special kind of arrogance to believe that justice is also merciful. This is why we are reminded many times throughout the Bible to "plead the cause of the poor and the afflicted," for this is the very heart of God.

Evangelicals embrace the idea that everything in life is a choice. Everything. I remember being lectured by a Christian friend after rehab and entering into Alcoholics Anonymous that if I could trace back my life, I would discover that at some point I had made a decision to sin and that while it may have been imperceptible at first, eventually the different path I had chosen separated farther and farther from the path of God. This is a form of logic that begins at the wrong place and presents a very simplistic, black and white, all or nothing view of life. Armed with this logic, it's easy to understand how, to Christians, everything that doesn't match their path is sin, to which the answer is always Jesus. One is either for or against, and there is no middle ground.

In this sense, evangelicals make perfect Republicans, for many conservative political beliefs flow from this same kind of logic. Welfare is a good thing only insofar as it directly aids the poor, but when, in their judgment, it becomes a crutch for those who are otherwise able (to get a job), it falls into the category of sin. Never mind all of the other factors contributing to poverty; if you only celebrate those who through whatever means find a way out of the quagmire, you're going to misfire on this highly complicated cultural issue. To turn our backs on poverty, because our core belief is that the poor are somehow faking it, is a violation of our calling as a religious people.

But it fits so well with Republican Party beliefs that Christians are easily drawn to the extreme edges of the party's right wing.

There used to be a political being known as the conservative Democrat. "Boll weevils" in the South helped Ronald Reagan pass his tax cut plan in the early 1980s. Before that, there were Dixiecrats and other groups. Pat Robertson's own father was a conservative Democrat. In the late twentieth century, "Blue Dogs" became their congressional moniker, and they represented mostly the poor people of the South. These are now completely aligned with the GOP, because followers now feel that Republicans better support their Christian views of life, primarily regarding public schools, abortion, and homosexuality.

This is remarkable, if you think about it, because rural Southern people are hardly representative of the societal business elite, those who have traditionally been the base of the Republican Party. When arguing against so-called "liberal Democrats," Reagan called them "tax and spend" liberals, meaning they wanted to take "your" money and use it for social programs that would benefit the have-nots. If one honestly examines this premise, however, those most concerned about having "their" money taken away are those who not only have it but will be the ones to lose the most dollars with the programs of liberals. They are the modern-day Pharisees, who preach a form of religion but actually serve the "gods" that gave them wealth. A perspective that points this out would truly represent a Biblical worldview, but that was not the case with us at the ministry of CBN. No one should ever feel ashamed of voting for a Democrat. No one.

Personal income was one of the major themes of the ministry of CBN. The idea that God wants His people to prosper in all ways—and especially financially—is based on an interpretation of certain scriptures, including John's letter to Gaius, also known as 3 John. Here's Chapter 1, Verse 2, in the King James translation: "Beloved, I wish above all things that thou mayest prosper and be in health, even as thy soul prospereth." Since Christians are God's beloved, this appears to be a message straight from God to believers and is open to interpretation as wealth. In the New Living Translation, however, it's presented thusly: "Dear friend, I hope all is well with you and that you are as healthy in body as you are strong in spirit." Now, I'm not a deep expositor of scripture, but the letter is from John to Gaius, and the verse clearly is John's greeting to him and not a message from God to certain believers.

Other references include the Old Testament, wherein God teaches the Jews how to prosper. In passing these along to Christians, however, there are significant intellectual streams that must be breached in order to wind up with instructions to contemporary Christians, including the reality that God made provision within the law to prevent the kind of wealth that exists with the few today. The Year of Jubilee—the ancient Jewish resetting of the economy—has been conveniently removed from modern times; for it would do the opposite of providing vast wealth for the few.

And yet, we chose stories of prosperity for the ministry only of people who met our criteria. They were young. They were good looking. Their testimony provided a witness that others would wish to emulate. They always ended up on top. They were always prospering after giving to CBN. In this way, we presented the tilted view that those who gave money to CBN—the greater the donation, the bigger the blessing—were always blessed by God. We didn't dare go near anyone who could claim the opposite, regardless of the reason.

One of the brightest and most talented producers on the staff of *The 700 Club* was Jon Simpson. Jon is now a world-traveler who documents with his video camera various ministries around the globe. He's brilliant today, and he was brilliant back then. Jon also had a gift in that he could do a very good interpretation of David Letterman's shtick in the field with everyday people. We were always looking for platforms that would allow for Pat to teach. One year I gave Jon the idea to create a franchise involving a well-intentioned Christian character that always got things wrong. It was comedic and a great platform from which Pat could then teach people about the errors the character had made.

Jon created a pilot in which his character tried to use the Law of Reciprocity (from Pat's *Secret Kingdom* that referenced "Give and it shall be given unto you") in order to pay his bills. If he needed one-hundred dollars, he would give ten dollars, and so forth. He wound up deeper and deeper into debt and finally gave up, looking at the camera and asking with arms outstretched, "What am I doing wrong?" I thought it perfectly represented what we were trying to create, and I was very proud to show it to Pat. It was funny. It was right on, because we knew that this was one of the trouble spots for people in living out their Christian lives.

Pat Robertson was not amused, not in the least. He stared at the screen as I played Jon's tape. We were alone in the dressing room, and I grew more uncomfortable the longer his eyes didn't blink. When it was done, he looked at me and said, "If you put this on the air, it will cost this ministry millions." He explained that we were all about helping people with their faith, and we dared not put anything in the show that might—not would, might—produce the opposite. I was instructed to never go near the subject again and to kill the franchise. I didn't need further instructions to know that this order was inviolable.

A similar rule was in place for testimony stories of physical healing, and it's here perhaps more than any other place that internal conflicts over right and wrong arose among the staff of the program. The person in charge of this aspect of the show was Karen Thompson, a talented and compassionate member of the team of producers and storytellers who also happened to be a nurse. Her task and the task of her staff was to filter through the myriad reports we received by telephone and turn them into as many "miracle" stories as possible. She was frustrated and so was I, because Pat Robertson's expectations most definitely didn't align with reality, especially given the restrictions we had on the types of people we could show on-the-air (young, not grossly overweight, smart, etc.).

In the spring of 1984, Pat objected to a miracle story that we had produced, saying it was too weak to put on the air. He reviewed every story in his dressing room prior to the program, and a big part of my job was to watch the videotapes with him and pass along his critiques, which could occasionally be quite brutal. I always filtered his comments, but sometimes his feelings would leak to the staff. Such was the case with this particular story, and Karen naturally objected. She sent me a memo out of frustration, and I was glad to take her case back to Pat. It relieved some of the pressure, but such things, like bugs in a kitchen, have a way of coming back. It didn't do much with Pat, and it didn't do much with my boss, Michael Little.

Here's some of what she said, and I want to reiterate that she was preaching to the choir in writing to me.

> I understand that you are going to ask Pat for written guidelines on what a miracle is. Good idea! But a word of caution—he will not be able to expect them in the quantity he wants to see. Will he be satisfied with fewer healing stories?
>
> I know that Pat believes, and I have heard him say on the air, that "thousands" of miracles are happening. The number of healing stories coming in to us does not correspond to his figure of "thousands." Many people who call in to the counseling center are simply claiming their healings & have seen no manifestation. Others have seen a brief manifestation, but then "lost" it (and these people are writing in more frequently asking what went wrong... they are confused and want to know why). Others write in enthusiastically (and this is VERY often) about their "miracle" and even provide us with medical documents. The medical documentation, however, usually reveals that there is far too much medical involvement (radiation, medication, etc.) for us to call it a miracle, or for skeptics to believe it was a miracle.

My department has become quite frustrated, Terry. I have always taken pride in my work and have tried to be conscientious in doing a good job. However, I'm experiencing frustration because the area of healing is out of my hands. I can only provide stories when God has done the healing. I can't do the healing myself. I hope that Pat does not feel I am keeping healing stories from him. I think you know how hard we search for them. I will do the best I can find them, but the rest is in God's hands. I cannot make up the stories.

Karen included documentation of what she had said, and this is what we were never allowed to present on the air. Remember, Pat saw our task as one of building faith even if we had to stretch the truth. Hence, our mandate was to show that God was busy doing miracles today just as He had in the days of Jesus. In the first quarter of 1984, we received 6,207 "Answer to Prayer" forms from the counseling center. We routinely asked people to call us on the air, and this was one of the categories. Karen's staff evaluated those and sent out follow-up forms to those that appeared promising. Of those 6,000 calls telling us about "miracles," we sent a little over 1,200 forms. From those, we had received just 290 responses, and that is where Karen's staff actually began their work. We had a staff of nurses who would follow-up and an advisory board of doctors who would "approve" reports before we ever did the actual stories. After filtering out the cosmetic rejections, that left very few we could put on the air with any confidence as to their veracity, sometimes as few as just one or two out of 300.

When you watched a healing testimony story during my time as producer of the program, both Karen and I were confident that it involved something mysterious or beyond physical explanation.

Pat's favorite healing stories were those that came about directly as a response to the time of prayer on the program. As practitioners of the gifts of the spirit as described in the book of Acts, Pat, Ben and Danuta sought grace for "words of knowledge" about those viewers who were in prayer over one thing or another, including healing. They would then speak out what they were "getting" from the Spirit in the hope that the person for whom it was intended would claim it in faith so that God could work a miracle. It all sounds pretty "out there," but for us, it was just every day ministering. In the very best of cases, storytellers could link an individual miracle back to a specific "word of knowledge," so that we could use videotape of the prayer along with telling the story.

This made it very easy and inspiring to then lead into further prayer, for the stage had been set in the hearts and minds of both the hosts and the viewers. Assuming a certain degree of skepticism among the readers here, let me say that, as a journalist, I was witness to many things that happened on the program that I could not explain. Doubters will doubt no matter what, and my job here is simply to present the facts of what happened, not convince anybody that the hosts of *The 700 Club* had a direct line to God in the handing out of miracles. That said, one day the hosts were in prayer and Pat said (paraphrasing), "Somebody's watching in prayer. There's a little boy named Mike or Mikey that's in trouble.

I can't tell exactly what it is, but I'm seeing something like a sash across his chest." He gestured the angle of this sash and continued, "God wants you to know that He's involved in this and that everything is going to be okay."

Later that day, the ministry received a praise report from a family in Pennsylvania, I think it was, that we investigated thoroughly and later produced a testimony story about to document their "miracle." It was truly remarkable. The husband was heading out to work and accidentally backed over his two-year-old son, Mikey, with the car. The boy had apparently tried to walk around the back of the vehicle to say goodbye to his dad and didn't make it. The father realized he was running over something when he hit a "bump," and he spun the tire over his son's chest in trying to get off. This left a bad burn on the boy's skin in the shape and angle of a sash. It matched perfectly the angle Pat had demonstrated during the time of prayer. They rushed Mikey to the hospital, where the whole family gathered and were in prayer as they were watching *The 700 Club* when this "word of knowledge" came during prayer. Miraculously, except for the burn, the boy was unhurt despite having been run over by a car! That story remains in my mind as *the* most unexplainable event in all the programs I ever produced. Everyone involved, including the family and their doctors agreed that something supernatural had taken place, and it had directly involved *The 700 Club*.

Even the most hardened "science only" skeptic would have to agree that this was at least unusual. I have no explanation other than it was what it was, an answer to prayer and not a "lucky guess" by Pat Robertson.

Despite this remarkable story, the truth is that these reports were not common, but the appearance that they were common was always our objective. We were dealing with the slippery concept of faith among our audience, and we were trying to stir the faith of individuals everywhere, so that they could claim results for themselves. This is a direct appeal of the gospel of self, especially for people in need for themselves, their families, their friends, their communities, etc. Presenting the suggestion that we had a hotline to God was also helpful in the extreme when it came to fundraising or offering Pat's political views, for who could argue with somebody capable of bringing about miracles like that? These prayers were, however, a somewhat divisive segment of the program, for so-called "words of knowledge" are a controversial theological concept within denominational Christianity.

Moreover, the relentless emphasis on a God that was "always" healing had a very dark downside, and that was with those viewers who were never healed and had no explanation. I got a letter late in my first season with the ministry, and it was one of the factors in my decision to leave in 1986 as Pat was beginning his run for president. It came from a father in Indiana. He and his family were members of a faith church—where belief in miracles often influence medical care—and regularly watched *The 700 Club*. He ripped into me for producing a program that always showed people getting healed, because his nine-year-old daughter had just succumbed to cancer. "Worse," he wrote, "than the agony of her suffering with the cancer towards the end, was the rejection she felt from God, because He wouldn't heal her."

"She watched your program every day," he went on, "and was ever full of faith that she would be healed based on the stories you showed. In the end, she felt an abandonment and rejection like few have ever known, and she cried constantly in shame that God didn't love her, because He was letting her die. She came to this belief by watching *The 700 Club*," he concluded, "and I will never forgive you for that."

This letter affected me deeply. I cried not only alone but also with others over what this little girl had suffered, and while we all could come up with justifications, we knew that the father was right. To this day, I pray for that little girl and her family and beg forgiveness for playing a role in what she went through.

Fortunately, these kinds of letters weren't commonplace, but the fear that we were manipulating people into believer status by bending the truth of miracles in such a way was omnipresent, not only for me but also for others on the staff who were in the trenches trying to deliver the sometimes-merciless demands of our leader. We spoke of immutable spiritual "laws" of God's kingdom that people "should" follow to be in sync with God's will. We read Answer to Prayer forms live on the air without vetting anything. This further advanced the narrative that God was moving mightily among us, as we invited viewers to experience it with us. The lines we regularly blurred were trouble to many of us, but we didn't speak out. We dared not, for the benefits of participation in what we were taught to believe was happening outweighed the possibilities that we were actually doing people harm.

Of the many hundreds of programs I produced with Pat Robertson, only once did we go even close to a theme that was something other than cheerleading for faith. That was a program about death, complete with stories of people who had experienced deep loss but found ways to overcome lasting blame or anger with God. This was a fantastic program and everyone on the staff felt it was among our very best. Pat, however, was uncomfortable throughout the show, although his prayer and teachings were among the most memorable ever. That program blessed many thousands of people, but it was the only time we ever broached the topic of things seemingly going wrong with God. Jesus always rescued people from despair on our program and always healed everybody. That we mixed in public Christian participation in the political process seemed oh so easy to accept as a part of the spiritual whole. After all, if *The 700 Club* said it, God must be involved, right?

And who doesn't want a miracle for themselves, whether that is physical healing, wealth, or any form of success? As long as the self was at the center, we were able to move people to action in one form or another. The gospel of self was our real message, and it was spoken in both subtle and obvious ways.

The 700 Club was one of the most thoroughly researched and smartly marketed television programs I've ever been associated with. In my life as a news director, my nickname was "Captain Statistics," because I loved research and was very good at interpreting results and creating strategies based on numbers. At CBN, we employed every contemporary research method in helping shape the program to our wants and needs while respecting the intelligence of viewers and especially potential viewers.

I remember specific instances where I really learned something. For one, we were able to prove that the television news practice of short stories and lots of them was not a scientific reality when it came to presenting compelling TV. I can recall a six-and-a-half minute story that we played for a theater filled with people who held dials in their hands that they could use to tell us in real time if what they were seeing was interesting. Every single person in that crowd continually raised their dials as the story progressed, and the interest was remarkably high even at the very end. This revealed to me that it isn't the length of the video story that determines interest; it's the content and especially the storytelling ability of the producer.

In the same session, we learned that the segment of the program that featured Pat, Ben, and Danuta praying for healing was vastly more controversial than we suspected. This was an exercise in the "gifts of the spirit," and the practice was generally regarded as extreme in the minds of most believers. It is in the same category as those who handle rattlesnakes in services without being bitten, although that practice is certainly at the farthest end of the category. Believing that God speaks to and through certain individuals with messages of knowledge about those being healed is not something most Christians are comfortable with practicing. Nevertheless, it was one of our daily segments. It's what led to the Answers to Prayer telephone calls, which led to the stories we produced, which led to the prayer segments; wash, rinse, and repeat.

This is why it was so fascinating to watch a room full of Christians react to what they were seeing. The segment was absolutely polarizing; people either loved it to one end of the dial, or hated it to the opposite end. There was zero in between. It was one of the most remarkable evidences of polarization via television that

I had ever witnessed, and even to this day, I've not seen anything like it.

At one of many focus groups we conducted, a man described the program perfectly as "progressively subjective," meaning that the show evolved to a more religious message as the minutes ticked by. We adopted this as an astute observation of the outline of our format, because it so perfectly fit actual practice.

Pat Robertson was a living dichotomy, at times charismatic, demonstrably authoritative, and a powerful, powerful presence. At other times, however, he could be the most human of souls. Like when we played tennis at The Homestead or elsewhere. I am fifteen years younger and a club trophy tennis player, but Pat never gave up in his attempts to beat me. I simply kept the ball in play and let him make the mistakes. Always the competitor, he wanted me to team up with him in doubles, but we never had the opportunity. He would laugh and let his frustration be evident during our games, and at those times, he was much more a friend than a boss.

I remember one morning when he showed up in the dressing room mumbling under his breath and blabbing incoherent words. "What's wrong?" I asked him. He went on to complain about the Ford Motor Company and how their ads were dishonest and misleading. He had a new Ford Bronco and had apparently taken it for a drive similar to what was shown on TV, with the vehicle bouncing through off road terrain and splashing through deep mud and puddles. He had messed up the brakes and the suspension on his new car, and wasn't happy. It was one of the funniest moments I ever had with him.

I was on the stage with Pat during our Friday prayer meetings and every other all-staff prayer gathering. I played my guitar and led worship with another guitar player, Bill Borowik, and Pat always expressed his love and admiration for our work. On September 6, 1983, Pat was even inspired to send a memo to Bill and me.

Just another word to tell you how outstanding the Labor Day prayer meeting was. I think the music was the best we ever had. The new faculty staff at the University was absolutely thrilled at the praise unto the Lord.

Thanks again,
PR

It was a real honor to lead worship at CBN, and as long as Pat was happy, I didn't really care what anybody else had to say. I was often asked to mix in more contemporary music, but those songs never seemed to fit in with what Bill and I were doing, which was to simply be guided by the flow. This required a certain simplicity to the music in order to follow one song with another in rhythm and take the praise and worship where we felt it needed to go. This meant no pre-planned list or order, because we didn't wish to tie ourselves into a set plan. We preferred to wing it, and the audience and Pat seemed to appreciate that. Nobody will ever know if Bill and I were being guided by our own egos or from beyond, but I do remember some remarkable times and feelings of utter bliss in the process of playing my guitar and singing in front of the staff of CBN.

I do remember a prayer meeting during which a woman began speaking in tongues in a moment of quiet. Pat immediately grabbed me and said, "Start playing something *now!*" I started playing and singing and Pat joined in at the same moment. Bill picked up on it, and soon the whole place was filled with song, and the woman was completely drowned out. This was the only time in the hundreds of prayer meetings I can recall that someone other than Pat brought what she believed was a "message" to the gathered. Afterwards, I asked Pat why he had interrupted her, and he said, "She was in the flesh," which meant he had interpreted her gesture as self-centered. I asked if he wanted me to always react that way, and he responded that it depended on who was prophesying and a discernment of the spirit. Fortunately, I never had to make such a decision.

There was one prayer meeting I recall that led to shameful behavior on my part, although it is very hard to admit. It was one of the holiday meetings, so everyone was present. I woke up that morning, sat on the toilet, and immediately threw my back out. It was awful, and I couldn't move very well. I was in intense pain as the relentless muscle spasms impacted nerves to the point where I was convinced I should stay home. I called Pat to apologize, and he would hear none of it.

"Come on, brother," he chided me. "Don't you think God can heal that?"

I went to the prayer meeting and stood there with Bill proclaiming praise to God Almighty, even though I was bent and twisted due to the constant pain. At one point, Pat stopped the music and told those gathered that I had hurt myself and needed healing. He directed those gathered to offer encouragement and to pray with him as he prayed for me. I set my guitar aside and joined him, as he placed one hand on my back and another on my forehead and began praying. He prayed that God would heal me immediately. He rebuked Satan. And when he closed with "in Jesus' name, amen and amen," the crowd erupted in applause and noise, as everyone prayed as they saw fit.

Pat looked at me and asked, "How do you feel?" I beamed a big smile and said, "Great, I feel just great!" He instructed me to reach down and touch my toes several times, and I did as he asked. The place went nuts as they witnessed this, what appeared to be a miracle. I picked up my guitar, and Bill and I broke into an upbeat tune as I danced that special dance that certain Christians know so well, rocking back and forth and kicking my legs forward and back. Praise the Lord! Or not.

The aching in my back was incredible, but I wasn't about to admit it. I tried to relax, but I couldn't. The spasms continued unabated. At the end of the meeting, I had to rise and play some more, but I never let on. After all, I had been healed, right?

I went home to my heating pad and babied myself for the next couple of days until the back pain went away. I used Pat Robertson's own thinking about faith to rationalize my deception. It was better to do that, I reasoned, than to harm anybody else's faith. Oy.

I tell this story, because I want to be honest about how far over the line of reason I was willing to go in order to support the narrative of Evangelical Christianity. I have discovered later in life that I'm not alone in faking things so as to look like I was as righteous as the next guy. I don't and won't accuse any of my

CBN contemporaries of such misrepresentation, for perhaps they are right, and I'm wrong in my views that God doesn't necessarily answer prayer that way. I've seen a lot of strange things in my life—things that I couldn't explain logically—but I know that when the faith chips were down for me, I failed the test miserably. I honestly believe today that it wasn't my unbelief at play in missing "my miracle" that day at CBN; it was much more a matter of honestly not feeling a bit different coming back up after I had bent down to touch my toes. It just wasn't there, and yet, my ego wouldn't permit exposure, so I simply faked it.

I have no doubt there are thousands of people today who fake things in order to be accepted by the church. It comes with the territory, for the need to look good in front of peers is one of the most compelling drivers of bad behavior in the world today. We don't stop being human just because we proclaim the name of Jesus, and thousands are leaving the church today over real or perceived contrary expectations presented by others in the name of love.

David Hayward is a lifelong member of the Christian faith, coming up in both ecumenical and evangelical churches. He went to a Pentecostal seminary and later a Presbyterian school. He served as a pastor for thirty years, before coming to a crossroads in his own heart over truth and the church. He is now known as "the Naked Pastor," a controversial cartoonist and commentator serving a wide variety of people and their beliefs in an ecclesiastical capacity online. He is both loved and hated in the Christian community for his unique takes on life and especially the church.

Here's a portion of a post, "Alarming Rate":

When people say that they are alarmed by people leaving the church, one has to conclude they're out of touch with reality. It's really not that alarming. It's not that complicated. It actually makes perfect sense.

To scold people who leave the church by saying that they just should go to church or that they are lost without it or that they've made a mistake and that it's their fault for leaving... it betrays a lack of self-reflection.

People are leaving the church for all kinds of reasons. They are...

- bored.
- fed up with being manipulated, coerced, and controlled.
- experiencing abuse and have had enough.
- not being challenged intellectually.
- being asked to believe unbelievable things against their consciences.
- looking for true community and are disappointed.
- desiring a freedom the church does not allow.
- giving up on the church's broken promise to make the world a better place.
- tired of being constantly violated spiritually, emotionally, intellectually, financially, etc.
- rejected, shunned, shamed, kicked out.

One of the reasons that Hayward doesn't mention is the volume of intolerance they hear, some from the pulpit but mostly from the congregation.

At CBN, while we prided ourselves in a scientific approach to marketing, as noted earlier, that marketing presented an unreal (fake) depiction of Christians in the United States. Pat Robertson used to say, "If you want to catch trout, you've got to use trout bait," which was a metaphor revealing a license to depict Christians in an ideal way rather than how Gallup's research had shown America described them. This was controversial in Virginia Beach and put unnecessary demands on those of us trying to fulfill the mission. Pat didn't interpret his own rules the same way we did, however, and this added to the confusion. Consider a letter Pat received in the summer of 1984 from a woman in Norfolk who somehow had heard about our rule of "no fat people" on *The 700 Club*. She was incensed, and Pat's letter back to her is revealing.

Dear Xxxxxxx,
Thank you very much for your letter. Sometimes things which are an expression of practical management turn into hard and fast law which may not be the intent at all.

Here's our problem. There are many Christians who are not just fat, but who are grossly obese. They don't smoke, they don't drink, and they don't run around, but the lust of the flesh focuses on their stomach. They make a poor testimony to those who are seeking to find faith. One person I read of said that after his experience with Christians, he presumed that he would "have to gain one hundred additional pounds to be like most of the Christians" he saw.

I would not be particularly anxious to put on the air a testimony of an alcoholic who was healed of the sickness but continued to be a drunk. I would like him both healed of his sickness and healed of his spiritual disorder as well.

I am sure that all the complex reasoning that goes into a decision does not get conveyed when it is passed down several levels. In any event, we are trying to draw men and women to Jesus, not repel them. Sometimes we do this imperfectly, but I feel that the reproach of the cross is hard enough without making the unbelievers feel they have to overcome the reproach of our own bad habits.

The way you explained "the policy" is, of course, indefensible. I do not believe that is the case.

Thanks for writing. With all good wishes, I am

Yours in Christ,

Pat Robertson
President

On my copy of the letter, Pat attached a note for my eyes:

If Xxxxxxx articulates what she understands as "our policy," it obviously sounds both unchristian and indefensible.

I believe that it should be reanalyzed, redefined, and especially rearticulated so that it makes sense in a Christian context. If it doesn't, then we should not have it.

This was very easy for Pat to say, but the proof of any CBN policy was in his dressing room prior to the program, where he said "yea" or "nay" to the videos I presented to him prior to the broadcast. His references to obesity as "sin" are reflective of general attitudes found among certain Christians and especially those of the evangelical right. The needy are always seen as being in sin, especially if they "could" help themselves. The problem, of course, is that obesity isn't necessarily sin, because there are contributing factors such as heredity, poverty, abuse, and others that get in the way of such a black and white view of life. *The 700 Club*, however, was Pat Robertson's ministry, and he has as much right to present his case as anybody else. Of course, he—and certainly people like me—are responsible and accountable for the results.

In many ways, the job of being Pat's producer was the proverbial "between a rock and a hard place." I found that the only way to survive was to be as flexible as possible to avoid the crush, and this meant being flexible in both directions, for I often became Pat's messenger, not only to my staff but also to other departments throughout the ministry. That dressing room could be a very difficult place to be, for Pat was fresh and ready to go. He often scooted off to lunches or other appointments immediately afterwards, and that left me to be his errand boy.

In many ways, Pat Robertson was an ambitious but benevolent autocrat, and a certain degree of fear was useful as such. He was so intelligent and his time such a limited commodity that arguing with him was largely a useless enterprise and one only to be used rarely. Adding to my stress was the knowledge that I would never receive adequate assurance from Pat that our political efforts were ethical and above reproach. Moreover, I was often called upon to explain that they were ethical to others who poked and prodded me, because they, too, couldn't express themselves to Pat personally.

In 1985, I began having vision problems in my right eye. There was an obvious blurring—a blind spot—that impacted my ability to see clearly. It was diagnosed as central serous retinopathy, also known as central serous choroidopathy, where a bubble forms in the back of the eye that interferes with vision. It's a serious medical problem, and for me, it produced scar tissue and is permanent. I will never see clearly out of my right eye. Here's what the American Academy of Ophthalmology has to say about it:

> Men are more likely to develop central serous choroidopathy than women, particularly in their 30s to 50s. Stress is a major risk factor. Some studies suggest that people with aggressive, "type A" personalities who are under a lot of stress may be more likely to develop central serous retinopathy.[6]

The stress of being Pat Robertson's producer in the time leading up to his bid for the presidency cost me the use of my right eye. Maybe it was more my inability to better respond to stress, but it doesn't matter anymore. The damage is done.

Thankfully, I usually had company in the dressing room during the viewing of the preproduced videos with Pat. Ben Kinchlow and Danuta Soderman joined the party, and both were well aware of the difficulties of trying to satisfy the mind of Pat Robertson. The lateness of the hour made long discussions impossible, and therefore, many decisions were snap judgments. Ben and

Danuta often functioned as a buffer, for their opinions, like mine, mattered to Pat. Our interactions could be, well, lively. It certainly wasn't a place for the faint of heart, however, and I learned much about how to stay calm during a confrontation from those regular encounters.

I am not a "natural" manager, but I turn management tasks into games in which I can compete and win. I discovered through my later studies an important paper written by Dr. Abraham Zaleznik for the *Harvard Business Review* in 1977, "Managers and Leaders: Are They Different?"[7] Managers accomplish tasks through organization and process, while leaders are capable of accomplishing tasks through the power of vision and character, including through what managers would view as chaos. Pat Robertson, for example, was not a manager according to Zaleznik's reasoning. Neither was I, which explains one of the key reasons we were able to connect so well. Managers, however, governed the ministry of CBN, and it was this more than anything else that caused me stress and its resultant gastroenterological health problems.

Ben and Danuta were also "leader" personalities, and that doubtless contributed to the amazing chemistry they had together as a team on television. Nonverbal cues are a vital part of behind-the-scenes communication for live TV, and I was extremely fortunate to participate with Pat, Ben, and Danuta on *The 700 Club*. I can't speak for what it's like today, but back then, it was quite remarkable to me. I loved that group, and I like to think that it showed both on the air and off.

Ben Kinchlow is one of the most likeable people I have ever encountered, and I don't know anybody who would argue with that. He is a giant teddy bear of a fellow who brought a street-smart wit to the chemistry of the team. His background as an African American was very different from Pat's upbringing as an American aristocrat, and that made for an entertaining interaction and one that was filled with mutual respect. The racial make-up of CBN in the early 1980s was almost entirely Caucasian. Ben's was the only black face on the management team, and his good-natured, self-deprecating humor often brought the house down, whether it was in the boardroom or on TV.

My roots are extremely modest, and I wince whenever I hear the popular politically correct term "privilege" when it's applied to me simply due to the color of my skin. I remember walking through the vast hall that is The Homestead with Ben one day during a *700 Club* retreat and observing the high society types being served by men and women dressed in white. The Homestead actually smelled of money, and as we walked along, I grew more and more uncomfortable with the place. I mentioned to Ben that I felt out of place. He stopped me and laughed.

"Man," he said, "if you feel out of place, imagine how I feel? Look at the people dressed in white! They're all black!"

Of course, he was right, and I felt embarrassed for even bringing it up. There are degrees of feeling out of place, and Ben had just trumped mine with a simple statement of truth. He was the only black face in the joint that was not wearing a white coat. We both laughed a belly laugh and got the hell out of there as soon as we could. I never went back inside the resort.

At that same retreat, I remember a fascinating discussion with Ben as we listened to the music of Aretha Franklin.

"Man," he looked at me and said, "You're a musical guy. Why does this stuff stir my soul, while Christian music just leaves me flat?"

He noted that Christian music, whether hymns, worship, or contemporary, spoke to his heart and that "entering into worship" always made him feel "good." However, pop music, especially soul music, touched him and spoke to him in a way that no other music did. It stirred his emotions and made him "feel" the message of the music. Ben thought it odd that music intended to minister to his soul just didn't do the trick. It's a great question even today.

The concept of ego among television personalities and other characters involved in live performances on any stage is vastly misunderstood. It is usually used to describe or justify bad behavior. People with "big egos" are generally regarded as irritating and often contemptible. This pejorative belief is unfortunate, for the behavior of ego-driven people is rarely a deliberate attempt to be difficult but rather a cover for real or perceived shortcomings. I've worked with hundreds of show hosts and anchors over the years, and I've found this to be universal. It takes an enormous ego to risk the significant potential embarrassment or worse of making mistakes on live TV. I find it easy to empathize with such because I am highly sensitive to the same thing. It tends to drive people to incredible heights in a constant search for acceptance.

Pat Robertson was very good at covering any potential nervousness about anything, but he had one very obvious "tell" in his behavior when backed into a potential corner. He would laugh to brush aside emotions in order to think more clearly and deliver an intelligent response. This laugh wasn't as genuine as Pat would,

I'm sure, like it to have been, and it was highly recognizable to anyone who spent a lot of time with him. Whether he was being interviewed on a live news program, involved in controversial discussions on *The 700 Club*, or even in certain business settings within the ministry, he would chuckle. When the chips were down in the moment, Pat would find a reason to laugh in order to delay his response. I always felt it was pretty smart, though it could be annoying. If you ever witness Pat Robertson chuckling at what seems to be an inappropriate moment, rest assured that he's uncomfortable and that the wheels of that magnificent mind are turning rapidly.

It is important for me to state at this point that despite the stress, the manipulation, the twisted mission, and other negativity noted here, my years at CBN were a net positive—and by a mile. The people, especially those who were a part of the staff of *The 700 Club*, were the most talented and committed people I've ever worked with. They are beautiful inside and out, and we had a great deal of fun during the years I was there. Any live television show produces a very real enemy in the clock, for it is a ruthless taskmaster that never quits. Consequently, there was a lot of humor involved in our work, the kind that you might find with a MASH unit in a time of war.

One day as a gag I wore an old necktie that I knew would draw a comment from Pat in the dressing room. He was such a stickler for quality ties, and this one was awful. It was a burgundy, pleated thing that resembled the type of curtain found in perhaps a funeral home. It was butt ugly, and I knew it. Pat practically gagged when he saw the tie and told me to take it off. I declined, which resulted in later hilarity on the set, as Pat couldn't stop complaining about it. I said it was an heirloom that I treasured.

I wore it again the following week just to rile him up, and it worked. The next time I wore it, however, he called me over to the set as a video story was playing, produced a pair of scissors, and cut it in half just below the knot. I was crestfallen while everybody in the studio got a good laugh, including the audience.

After shopping for some Velcro, I reattached the pieces of the tie. It was now a pull-away tie that created a nice tearing sound when pulled from the bottom. I showed up with it, and Pat about split a gut laughing. He must have ripped that tie a dozen times during the program. I still have it today, and it remains one of my most prized possessions.

I was also witness to some of the most fascinating interviews with people who played significant roles in history. In my years as producer, the most memorable guest was Dr. Benjamin Mays, one of the founders of the Civil Rights Movement. Mays was almost ninety when he appeared on the show, but he was remarkably alive, and his mind was crystal clear. He was an author, educator, former president of Morehouse University, a pastor, and one of the leading authorities on the black church in America. One statement he made in that interview was burned into my consciousness where it remains today. Pat asked Dr. Mays what he thought was wrong with young people today. Dr. Mays replied, "Parents are extraordinarily afraid to let their children experience the same kinds of things that shaped their own character." It was a remarkably perceptive argument back then and a bold statement of truth.

I will also never forget the appearance of pop star Donna Summer in 1983, at the very pinnacle of her success. We received word that she would be interested in discussing her faith with us, if we could come to California to do the interview. It would be the first time she had publicly discussed her background and faith in such an intimate way. Our guest services coordinator Jackie Mitchum met with line producer Christina Rylko and me to discuss the matter. I can't recall who came up with the idea, but we were all very excited about the possibility of taking the whole program to Hollywood for a week. Pat gave a nod to the idea, and I went to Los Angeles to survey possible site locations for the broadcast, while Jackie and Christina roughed out the plans.

We ended up at Universal Studios, where we got the red carpet treatment from everybody involved. Major celebrities with testimonies of faith were scheduled, but it was Donna Summer who headlined everything. Known as the disco queen, Miss Summer was prolific at that time in cranking out *Billboard* chart toppers. She was as famous as it gets, and it would be unfair to compare her success with anybody today. She was warm and gracious and eager to tell her story.

Just before her interview, I had to run to the Universal office to tend to a matter, so I didn't get back until the interview was nearly completed. That walk back to our studio on the grounds of Universal was unforgettable. Every room, every office, and every window I passed had its closed-circuit TV set tuned into *The 700 Club*. People were gathered around watching Donna Summer, because the studio had spread the word that she would be on live TV telling intimate details of her past. It gave me such a sense of community and a real blessing as I made my way back to our set. It was without a doubt the most memorable event of my television career, and the series of programs from California received accolades from every corner of the Christian world, broadcast or otherwise.

I need to pause here to pay respect to Christina Rylko, whose hard work and dedication eased the burden I felt as the show's producer. Christina was a young and beautiful woman with smarts, grace, and skill far beyond her years. She charmed everybody while kicking ass, but her competence is what I will always remember. She was one of the very few people I've worked with in my career that I could trust completely to regularly crank out excellence in the execution of her duties. She could read my mind and turn any vision into great television. She was rare, and Pat loved working with her, too. I owe her—and, frankly, the whole staff—a great debt of appreciation.

Four

The Shadow Government, 1984–1985

If you want to catch trout, you have to use trout bait.
—Pat Robertson

There's an old joke that suggests there are three people the devil doesn't want in hell: Billy Graham, because he would get everybody saved; Oral Roberts, because he'd get everybody healed; and Pat Robertson, because he'd raise the money for air conditioning.

We took in $248,000,000 in contributions during 1984, in what turned out to be a record for the ministries of CBN. That's an enormous sum of money even by today's standards—over half a billion in 2016 dollars—but thirty years ago, it was astounding. There were several single days in which donations exceeded a million dollars. By any stretch of the imagination, this was a phenomenal human accomplishment. Our belief prior to the scandals that rocked the whole religious broadcasting industry in subsequent years was that this level of "revenue" would continue, because, well, "God could!"

All that money was viewed as a blessing from God and validation that we were in His will in everything we set our hands to accomplish. Who could question that? After all, Pat Robertson's book *The Secret Kingdom,* which we had used as a donor premium (our "free gift" for their contribution), spelled out the "laws" of God's Kingdom, and we followed them completely. Surely, we felt, this was Pat's "Law of Reciprocity" at work—"Give, and it shall be given unto you; good measure, pressed down, and shaken together, and running over, shall men give into your bosom. For with the same measure that ye mete withal it shall be measured to you again."[8]

I would like to be able to say in truth that all of that money was used for righteous purposes, but I can't. Most of it went to running the ministries of a television network with over 2,000 employees, but some went to our foreign ministries, such as operating a radio station in southern Lebanon, and that had both political and missionary motivations; some went to political activities, such as funding the Freedom Council; and some went to interfering with government policies, such as helping fund the Contras in Nicaragua.

We were continuously emboldened to take on political issues as well, and our voice turned many to the Republican Party. The concept of the conservative Democrat faded quickly, as we relentlessly painted Democrats—all Democrats—as a liberal enemy that was after everybody's money. Our slogan—*TV Journalism With A*

Different Spirit—was the precursor of Fox News, and the "Biblical worldview" that we offered seemed to hit home with a growing number of evangelicals. This worldview, however, was overflowing with conservative political perspectives, largely because political conservatives—the Republicans—seemed most likely to embrace our point-of-view. They were with us on abortion. They were with us on prayer in schools. They were with us on Israel, and many, many other issues. Fox News would never have found the success it has known if CBN News hadn't blazed the trail. And while he gave News Director Mike Patrick and his brilliant staff a lot of room within which to operate, make no mistake: Pat Robertson was the editor, publisher, and thought leader of CBN News.

One of the required prayer meetings at CBN took place each year on New Year's Day, and 1984 was no exception. We had a terrific benefits package at the ministry when I first joined, so nobody ever complained about holiday participation in prayer. With my musical background as a singer-songwriter, I was blessed to lead worship at these all-staff meetings. They were terrific prayer meetings with upwards of 1,000 in attendance, an intense time of worship and music, and followed by a special message from Pat Robertson, communion, and, of course, prayer. Pat's tradition at year's end was to seek God in prayer at his mountain retreat home in Hot Springs, Virginia, at The Homestead resort. At the beginning of 1984, Pat came back from the mountain with the message from God that the year would be one of "deep darkness and trouble" for the nation, and we followed that theme throughout the whole year on *The 700 Club*, especially when it came to fundraising. The theme of our record-setting telethons that year was "deep darkness and trouble," and the evidence that it really did resonate with our viewers was their $248 million in contributions.

Here's a version of this prophecy that Pat shared with *The 700 Club* audience during a "Can of Worms" question segment on December 30, 1983:

> I've been in prayer. I put this out as what I feel God is telling me. Here's what I see in 1984: Toward the end of 1984, there will be a period beginning of deep darkness on our nation. I believe that we're going to have a time of trouble. There will be some leadership shifts in our nation. Those who begin to get involved will be those who are walking in darkness. They will not have the light of life. Yet at the same time, God said "I'm going to give light on my people, and the world will know that I can make a difference between those that are mine and those that are not."
>
> And I believe that there may be convulsions in the world, shifting of leadership in a number of nations. As the shifts in leadership take place, there's going to be a call for Christians to understand how the system works and to prepare for sort of a general collapse. I think this financial thing has not gone away. It may be into 1985, but the trigger is going to come, I think, towards the end of '84.
>
> Deep darkness and trouble—but on the people of God, light.
>
> And to God's people, God will give wisdom, and He's going to give solutions to them just like He did to Daniel and to Joseph and those people who found favor in God's

sight. Even so, those who found favor in God's sight are going to be given wisdom, and we will understand the solutions to the world's problems. And so the world is going to start coming and saying, "You've got something we don't have." But in order to do something, I believe the call upon the Church in 1984 is earnest prayer.

Get your own house in order. Remember what happened to Noah. As there gets to be trouble, get your own house in order financially and spiritually. Walk with God. In your financial structure, stay out of debt. Beware of the debt trap of the easy credit thing that's coming on our earth, and everybody gets all loose and realizes there's an impending financial disaster looming in the wings. Stay out of debt, especially this credit card, easy debt you can get into. And be prepared, but more than anything, spiritually. And I think we need to have earnest prayer in the Church and the people of God to avert some of the things that may be happening.

Possibly, if we all pray together, God will hear and take away some of the evil. But unless something like that happens, deep darkness and trouble.

As it turned out, 1984 wasn't really all that bad in the US. The AIDS virus was identified, but that was seen as a medical breakthrough. Michael Jackson's hair caught fire while filming a Pepsi commercial, but he went on to win eight Grammys a month later. McMartin Preschool teachers were charged with satanic ritual abuse of schoolchildren in a case that outraged everybody.

However, after ruining many lives, all charges were found to be
wholly unfounded and false. The Soviets boycotted the Olympics,
which likely hurt the economy of Los Angeles but nowhere else.
It was a good year for NASA. We did have our share of natural
disasters, the economy was just lumbering along, urban crime was
on the upswing and crack cocaine began its ripple effect among
mostly the poor and disenfranchised. But what about that "towards
the end of the year" of which Pat spoke?

Coincidentally, there was another significant event occurring
that fit perfectly into this view of God's warning about deep darkness and trouble. Ronald Reagan was running for re-election, and
to nearly everyone in the evangelical world, Reagan was seen on a
level of the righteous kings of old Israel. In 1984, CBN Executive
Vice President and Chief of Staff Bob Slosser published his tenth
book, *Reagan Inside Out,* in which he told the story of one particular prophecy made about and for Ronald Reagan when he was
governor of California in 1970. This book was offered to Christians
in an election year to help remind them of the president's Christian
upbringing, roots, thinking, and, of course, the prophecy. The
book jacket notes that Slosser's "searching description of the presidential personality and his analysis of the president's faith will be
welcome information to everyone who genuinely cares about our
nation, under God."

The men who prophesied over Reagan in 1970 were deeply
loved and admired friends of Pat Robertson's, men who advised
and prayed with him regularly and were viewed with a form of profound reverence and respect among the employees of the Christian
Broadcasting Network and its affiliate organizations. Chief among

these were Lutheran pastor Harald Bredesen, a man revered by the entire CBN community; George Otis, the founder of Christian radio and television in the Middle East, Voice of Hope; and singer Pat Boone. Bredesen and Otis, whom Boone considered his "two Holy Spirit fathers," profoundly influenced him and his career.[9]

Here is an excerpt from the opening chapter "A Prophecy" from Slosser's book *Reagan Inside Out*:

> Seven sharply different people drifted into that moment on this Sunday afternoon in October 1970, stepping almost aimlessly toward the foyer of a stately Tudor home in Sacramento. They were talking rather softly, but running over one another's words as they edged toward the entrance.
>
> One moved in front, then hesitated, looking back at the rest. That was Herbert E. Ellingwood. He was, in a fashion, herding four of the others, who were obviously visitors. He was just a whisper out of rhythm with them—not awkward, perhaps tentative. They were getting ready to say good-bye and that heightened everyone's uncertainty.
>
> Ronald Reagan was smiling and nodding as he turned his head toward Pat Boone, whose smile caused his entire face to glisten. Nancy Reagan watched the two of them momentarily, the barest trace of a smile on her lips, and then she whispered two or three words to Shirley Boone. Two rather short men, Harald Bredesen and George Otis, moved toward Ronald Reagan and Boone. Both were silent, and Bredesen seemed to be studying the floor.

Suddenly, everyone stopped. In the split-second of stillness, they looked at one another. Then one of the men—Boone or Bredesen—said, "Governor, would you mind if we prayed a moment with you and Mrs. Reagan?"

"We'd appreciate that." Reagan's face remained bright and pleasant but eased ever so slightly toward seriousness.

It was hard to tell who moved first, probably Boone, but in a sort of chain reaction, the seven took hold of each other's hands and made an uneven circle. For an instant, they were like little children, each looking first to the right and down at one set of hands and then left to the other. Only Boone seemed thoroughly at ease, but long friendship had broken all barriers between him and all those there, including the Reagans, their hosts. He had a happy smile on his face. Otis and Bredesen were obviously tense. Nancy's expression was quizzical but relaxed.

All seven closed their eyes. Reagan bowed his head sharply; Nancy's remained fairly level. The others tilted theirs a bit.

Otis, standing to Reagan's left, remembered the few seconds of awkward silence that followed. "It was a little tense," he said, "a bit embarrassing. We didn't know how they felt about doing that, you know. Suddenly we realized we might be a little presumptuous."

And that's the way they stood, holding hands, eyes closed. Otis thought the seconds seemed like minutes. He cleared his throat, and began to pray, "Lord, we thank you for the chance to be here together…" It was very general, the kind of prayer offered at large and small gatherings all across the land. It was so ordinary that no one remembered much of it.

"I was just sort of praying from the head," Otis said. "I was saying those things you'd expect—you know, thanking the Lord for the Reagans, their hospitality, and that sort of thing."

That went on for ten or fifteen seconds, and then it changed. "Everything shifted from my head to the spirit—THE Spirit," Otis recalled. "The Holy Spirit came upon me and I knew it. In fact, I was embarrassed. There was this pulsing in my arm. And my hand—the one holding Governor Reagan's hand—was shaking. I didn't know what to do. I just didn't want this thing to be happening. I can remember that even as I was speaking, I was working, you know, tensing my muscles and concentrating, and doing everything I could to stop that shaking.

"It wasn't a wild swinging or anything like that. But it was a definite, pulsing shaking. And I made a great physical effort to stop it—but I couldn't."

As this was going on, the content of Otis' prayer changed completely. His voice remained essentially the same, although the words came much more steadily and intently. They spoke specifically to Ronald Reagan and referred to him as "My son." They recognized his role as a leader of the state that was indeed the size of many nations. His "labor" was described as "pleasing."

The foyer was absolutely still and silent. The only sound was George's voice. Everyone's eyes were closed.

"If you walk uprightly before Me, you will reside at 1600 Pennsylvania Avenue."

The words ended. The silence held for three or four seconds. Eyes began to open, and the seven rather sheepishly let go of hands.

Reagan took a deep breath and turned and looked into Otis' face. All he said was a very audible "Well!" It was almost as though he were exhaling.

Otis was struck by the calm expression on Reagan's face. "I was really concerned about how he might have taken it all," George remembered. "But the expression on his face was kind, wholesome—a receptive look, you know. It was not gushy or sentimental or any of that. He just said, 'Well,' and that was that. We all said good-bye, and we left."

To fully appreciate the power of this prophecy in driving the early 1980s revival that the televangelists ushered in, readers must understand and accept the circle from which it came and that the wider circle included people such as Pat Robertson. We rarely spoke of it directly, but I knew as Pat's producer that this was a seminal moment in the development of the "latter rain" of which Bredesen spoke to Ronald Reagan that day. "Latter rain" is an idea taken from the King James translation of the Book of Joel, one considered prophetic to many evangelicals. It's an expression of an outpouring of The Holy Spirit that would be accompanied by signs and wonders, such as healing the sick, casting out demons, and speaking in tongues. These, of course, were standards of the CBN ministry and *The 700 Club*.

In a July 24, 2007 CBN obituary of George Otis, Craig von Buseck wrote that Otis had told *Charisma* magazine: "We realized we had heard the voice of God... Reagan acknowledged the prophecy to Boone after his first inauguration in 1981, indicating that he felt guided by a sense of divine purpose."

Slosser wrote of Reagan after the 1980 election, "Reagan was in the White House. The country loved him. His party held a majority in the Senate for the first time in twenty-six years. Republicans had gained the House and given that body a more conservative flavor. He said he was on God's side. God seemed to be on his."

In light of this providential view of history, it's easy to see how the risk of a Reagan defeat in November of 1984 would come across as the potential for "deep darkness and trouble," given the "fallen world" into which this group of evangelicals believed God had thrust Ronald Reagan as a righteous form of leadership for difficult times. There existed at CBN in 1984, a very strong and heady sense of purpose regarding what we felt was a significant movement of the Spirit of God across the land and that our foot was to remain heavy on the accelerator. Ministries were exploding with growth, and George Orwell's dystopian *1984* seemed less likely than a certain utopian view of ushering in God's kingdom. We rarely discussed it openly, but Pat's prophecies and the unfolding of events in the secular world made it easy to convince others and ourselves that something, perhaps an event, was approaching that would validate our work. Perhaps even the return of Jesus Christ Himself.

Another, rarely discussed influence on this "darkness" was that there was nobody of a righteous sort waiting in the wings to replace Reagan. George H. W. Bush, the vice president, was hardly the kind of man that evangelicals could really get behind. In fact, as former Reagan national security advisor Richard Allen wrote for the *New York Times* in 2000, Bush was the lesser of two evils for Reagan. Allen called Bush the "accidental" Vice President.

> There are many plausible versions of how and why Reagan chose George Bush as his running mate, but most are wide of the mark. One conventional view is that Reagan, about to be nominated, recognized that he "needed a moderate" like Bush to balance the ticket; another version has it that Reagan, supposedly unschooled in foreign affairs, saw the wisdom of naming someone with extensive experience in the field to offset his own shortcomings. Yet another explanation holds that Reagan, a Californian, needed "geographic balance" and got that in Bush, with his Connecticut and Texas lineage.
>
> I thought Bush a viable alternative to Ford; he had the best credentials of the possible running mates mentioned. If not for the unsettled relations between the two, Bush could bring more to the ticket to help Reagan than anyone on the list of choices.
>
> There was no question that a Bush candidacy would be a hard sell. Among Reagan's advisers, Nofziger and Casey viewed Bush as a liberal, and others were almost unanimously against him, some even contemptuous. I considered Bush a capable man whose positions were actually much closer to Reagan's than were Ford's, especially on foreign policy and defense matters…[10]

According to Allen, Reagan was never going to approve of the "shared presidency" proposed by Gerald Ford, so Bush was the best alternative.

The assassination attempt on President Reagan on March 30, 1981, sixty-nine days into his presidency, had raised the specter of a Bush presidency, and the thought didn't sit well with the evangelical crowd, who viewed him as a pro-abortion outsider and a long way from conservative. He had also ridiculed Reagan's economic policies as "voodoo economics" and his refusal to admit defeat for the nomination was regarded as willful and unnecessary, as suggested by Allen.

Pat told me he thought Bush was a dirty political player, something I would learn much more about later. The point is that there were many reasons for Pat to prophesy "deep darkness and trouble" in 1984, and they included uncertainty about his perceived need to keep the country moving in a conservative direction. Reagan *had* to be re-elected, and the time to deal with Mr. Bush would come later.

Pat Robertson loved Ronald Reagan. Perhaps it's more precise to say that he loved Reagan's beliefs in traditional values—"American values," he would call them—the kind that Pat felt the country needed to "make it great" again. During a discussion on *The 700 Club* in March of 2015, Pat nostalgically stated his wish that Reagan would "rise from the dead." The mere idea, therefore, that Bush would replace the president was unthinkable.

Robertson wasn't alone, of course, in this thinking. Many on the political right were beginning to look ahead and consider what to do in 1988. In an article in the *Washington Times*, writer Ron

Cordray broached the subject in 1985. "Combined with the emergence of evangelical political activists ..." he wrote, "New Right leaders ... fear a Republican slide to the left following the Reagan presidency." Cordray added, "Many conservatives, despite admiring him for his 'loyalty' to the president, are distrustful of Mr. Bush."

Of course, Ronald Reagan went on to win in a landslide in 1984. It broke presidential election records with the largest Electoral College victory in history. Reagan won forty-nine of fifty states. Only Walter Mondale's home state of Minnesota went in the blue column. The popular vote was likewise lopsided, with Reagan capturing nearly sixty percent of the voter ballots for president.

The banking crisis to which Pat Robertson had referred back in January and spoke about throughout the year did not really materialize in 1984, and that weighed on him as he again went away to the Virginia mountains to rest, pray, and seek God's insight for 1985. What he returned with was only partially revealed publicly on *The 700 Club* during its January 1 broadcast. The rest came in a private meeting later.

> **Pat:** We're on the knife's edge in terms of the banks. The executive vice-president of one of the major banks in Virginia told me just the other day. He said they're in much more critical shape than they were in '74 or '75. It's much worse, because of major energy loans, real estate loans, commodity loans, Third World Country debts, and, of course, the federal deficit that's out there. All of these things are very confusing to them.

Danuta: So do you think that 1985 will see a major crisis or just the brewing of one?

Pat: It could happen. It could be a break any time. You see, God's been so good to us. I mean, we've been kind of walking on borrowed time, but now we've got this $200 billion deficit. 1984: one thing happened that was very significant. 1984 marked the end of seventy years of United States positive balance toward the rest of the world. We became a debtor nation for the first time in seventy years. I mean, we've given up two generations of prosperity, if you want to look at it that way. And you can't keep living at the bank and borrowing. We're now in the hands of foreign forces that can dominate and control, unless God Himself does something. And so the economy is very, very fragile. There is no leverage for the Fed; there is no leverage for the federal government. They can't increase the deficit to inflate, because the deficit is already as high as it can be. They can't do anything with the Fed's policies to speak of, because it's out of their control. There's just nothing much that can be done with policy except to cut the budget tremendously, and nobody's willing to do that. So it seems like to me we're going to have a gridlock up there in Washington...

The other thing that's significant, Ben, is that God's people are coming to the fore. You know, God said we were supposed to be the head and not the tail. We're supposed to be on top and not on the bottom. And I think the long-range trend is that God's people are going to move into positions of leadership—I mean in all kinds of areas. I mean, there's going to be general growing prosperity and blessing for the people of God. Now that's my opinion, but I think that's going to happen. It's going to get better and better and better, and God's going to begin to thrust His people into positions they never dream they were capable of taking on. They're going to move into new areas of responsibility in the next few years. And I think the other thing that's going to happen definitely is the Soviet Union, that leadership over there. That country is going to be wracked apart. I don't know whether it'll be next year or the year after or the year after, ten years, but there's going to be an ultimate overthrow of some fashion, of that terrible, awful power that has been enslaving so many billions of people for so many years.

Ben: What should Christians begin to do?

Pat: I think if they haven't done it, they ought to start getting on their knees and praying for revival. I think the revival is going to be the key. We cannot just say, "Well, we're going to sit back and let it happen." We need to humble ourselves; we need to pray; we need to turn from our wicked ways; we need to seek the face of God. And he's going to hear from heaven and forgive our sins and heal our land. We need to pray for revival, to renew the prayer for revival, because good things are happening. I mean, it's like the Lord is saying, "Hold your hands out. I'm going to put it in your hand. Just hold your hands out. But get yourselves ready for it. Get together; work in unity; and pray and seek My face."

There's going to be a huge ingathering of souls. There's going to be an enormous amount of evangelism. And this is going to be one of the most exciting years and each year thereafter. I mean we're going to see some fabulous years. It'll be like a fairy story. It's going to be like we're listening to a fairy tale. We won't believe what's going to be happening. We will not believe it, but it's going to be happening. It will be very good. But economically we're walking on a knife's edge. We have been on it for the last couple of years. And only the grace of God has kept us from some kind of a terrible thing. It can happen; but so far, so good.

The January 1, 1985 program had been taped, so that CBN could have its annual New Year's Day prayer meeting. Pat spoke more about the vision there and, after the gathering, summoned a few of us to the conference room upstairs. The beautiful, wood-paneled room with an original old painting of George Washington on the wall, was usually either empty or full, but this time only four of us took seats near the head of the table. The atmosphere was somber but pleasant, although the air was thick with anticipation. It was unusual for Pat to gather key executives after a prayer meeting, and I was excited to hear what he had to say to us. Present, as I recall, were Bob Slosser, Michael Little, and myself.

After pleasantries were exchanged, we all sat there silent for a few seconds before Pat began.

He repeated what we had heard at the prayer meeting, that 1985 would be a bumpy road for the world but a year of tremendous blessing for "the church." Then, as I recall, his words drifted to higher thoughts:

"We must form a shadow government," he began. "We must begin to find and train Christian people, so that they can be placed in every position that matters, because the country is on the verge of collapse. The Lord is showing me that when it goes, nobody is going to know what to do, and they will turn to us, because we will have answers. We won't be afraid. We've got to work to make sure God's people are in the schools, the school boards, the city councils, the county commissions, the trash collectors, the tax collectors and all local government positions. We need to be in the state legislatures, the statewide offices, Congress, the courts, everywhere. We can't be overt and obvious about this; we must do it quietly and create this shadow government."

He did not share exactly how we were to do this, and I don't think anyone present had a real inkling at that point about how far downstream he was projecting this vision. Here's Pat on *The 700 Club* a week later:

> (The upcoming year is) going to be kind of like a bumpy road full of potholes and trouble. But it isn't necessarily going to be that you can't get from point A to point B. It's not going to be some cataclysm. But there's not going to be anybody, the Lord was telling me, in the world scene,

who's going to know the answers. In other words it's going to be a time of rather large confusion. There's going to be a divergence of opinion on so many things. And we'll have all these potholes. That means that some of the banks will be going down, and we'll be having spotty problems in our economy. I mean, it's not going to be like smooth sailing, and it's not going to be the end of the world. But it's going to be a difficult year, just like driving on a country road full of holes and potholes.

But in terms of CBN, it's kind of like all systems are go. God is blessing tremendously. This will be a better year than we had in 1984. It's going to just continue to— God's blessing is here. And He just kept ensuring me. But there were three or four scriptures that the Lord gave me specifically … The words had to do with pulverizing the ungodly. And, of course, we can't go out and pulverize people today, but I think the way you pulverize is in prayer. We cannot let up. And I think there's a tendency of the Christians to think, "Well, the election's over. Somehow '84 was a great something or other." But it wasn't …

We've got to wipe out the forces of evil; in prayer, in Bible knowledge, in evangelism and that kind of thing. There's got to be an effort like never before, especially in prayer for revival. And if there's one word, I would think, is the concept that the Church is getting ready to reign and rule. That is what God has in mind. He's going to exalt the mountain of the house of the Lord. And that has been a gradual process. It's going to be accelerated in this year and the next year and the next year. We're going to see God's people lifted up. But in order for them to be lifted up, in a sense, the wicked need to be removed from the land. And the way you do it in our way is to change the wicked so that they will become saints. And you do it through persuasion and through prayer and through revival. And that's what is God's plan and program, I think, in this coming year.

To prepare God's people for this reigning and ruling during or after this period of "confusion," Pat believed we needed to assist in creating a shadow government that would "take over" when everything collapsed. I had no idea how such a plan would be implemented, but I felt certain it would involve *The 700 Club*, so I made myself available for every meeting and every discussion moving forward. Still, Pat played his cards close to the vest. However, I got an indication of how this was unfolding in Pat's mind during our January telethon, when I was shown an advance copy of the March issue of the *Saturday Evening Post* magazine. Pat's picture was on the cover in one of those iconic drawings—this one by Lucian Lupinski—that traditionally adorned the covers of the *Post*.

Next to the picture was the headline, "CBN's Pat Robertson: White House Next?"

When I questioned him about it in private times back then, he told me it was just a trial balloon, that a lot of people had encouraged him to do so, and that he was "seeking God" on whether he should. I expressed to him (for the first time) that such a move would dramatically impact the ministry and *The 700 Club*, but he was already aware of these things. The article was merely a fleece, of sorts.

But I knew that this explanation was just a brush-off. Pat was very clear in his distrust of George H. W. Bush becoming President Reagan's replacement in 1988, so why not Pat himself? Moreover, the editor and publisher of the *Saturday Evening Post* was Dr. Cory SerVaas, a regular contributor to *The 700 Club*. She had a regular health and nutrition segment on the program that we taped, sometimes with Pat, during her regular visits to Virginia Beach. I could only wonder how long the article had been in the works. Given the planning cycle of magazines and the high-quality portrait by Mr. Lupinski, it was very likely in development many months before the advance copy had been made available to us. It was not simply a reaction to the "message on the mountain" that Pat had related to us at the beginning of the New Year in 1985.

In fact, Pat had been trying to encourage conservative Christians to get involved in the political process since at least 1981, when he formed the Freedom Council, a 501(c)(4) tax-exempt organization with the authority to lobby on behalf of political candidates. But the Freedom Council was a part of the CBN family, and as such it received attention on *The 700 Club* and especially during our telethons. The reality is that we used the 501(c)(3) tax-exempt status of CBN's ministries to raise money that went to the Freedom Council, and that was the basis of the IRS investigation triggered—I believe by George H. W. Bush—during Pat's run for the presidency.

During 1985 and 1986, according to the *New York Times*, we gave $250,000 a month or more to the Freedom Council "to mobilize Christian voters behind Mr. Robertson's candidacy for the Republican Presidential nomination in 1988." The total estimate reached as high as $8.5 million to the Freedom Council, according to the *Times*.[11]

Despite the fact that CBN reached a "significant" settlement with the IRS in March of 1998, the shadow government aspect of Pat's involvement in politics has been entirely overlooked by those who observe culture and write history's first draft. The popularity of Fox News may seem mysterious to some but not to me.

There were clearly two forces at work at *The 700 Club* in 1985. One was the mission of CBN as carried out with passion and skill by the staff and crew of the ministry. In all my years in television and television consulting, I have never worked with a brighter and more capable group of people than those who worked with me in Virginia Beach. I would put our work on a level with the very best in the secular television world, regardless of how far we tilted in one direction or another. TV is TV, and we made good TV.

The second force at work was conservative politics, headed by Pat Robertson himself. As mentioned earlier, Pat was a political strategist who happened to be a minister. Despite his passion for the gospel and evangelicalism, at core he was a political master with knowledge and ability beyond most. He could extemporaneously and intelligently discuss any matter involving any nation in the world. In his head, Pat Robertson contained more accessible knowledge than even, I believe, any US secretary of state. He studied the world. He was a voracious reader of international news reports. He had a strong ability to link foreign governments and to pull that knowledge out of his head at a moment's notice. This was the real Pat Robertson that I knew, which is why I felt that ministry was more an avocation than his true passion, which was politics.

This force moved to center stage in the 1984-85 period. It was unmistakable. I knew it, and I helped move *The 700 Club* in that direction. I did it because it was expected of me, but I also did it because I knew that history was somehow shifting. I felt feelings of rebellion and uprising that I hadn't felt since the counterculture movement of the 1960s, and I was proud to be a part of it. I knew the law well; especially broadcast law, and I knew how to skirt the edge of its limits. I also wasn't afraid to push the envelope, which was encouraging to Pat. Mostly, I knew how to take his direction and transform that into action as a media company.

In major meetings in the boardroom, which consisted of a couple of dozen white males plus Ben Kinchlow and Danuta Soderman, mine was one of the few heads that moved in both directions. When Pat would make a statement, you could count on nods from most of those present. Michael Little was ever the diplomat when he disagreed. Bob Slosser was always the soft-spoken and articulate executive when he could not agree. I was the onboard iconoclast, and Pat would often look at me for reaction in such situations.

One of the important things Pat Robertson taught me was to never fear the boss, and that has been my stock in trade ever since. In Ecclesiastes, it says, "If the anger of the ruler rises against you, hold your place; for deference makes amends for great offenses."[12] I am very grateful for what he taught me, and it was one of the reasons I felt such a sense of partnership with Pat during this time in the ministry. He needed my help in involving *The 700 Club* with his political views, and I gave that help willingly. It was rarely, however, discussed openly or freely with me, nor was I "ordered" to do so. It was much more natural than that, and I felt I was simply following my heart as senior producer of the program.

Despite the fact that the experience put an asterisk beside my name in the world of secular television, I've always told people that I did some of my very best work at CBN. I introduced world-class news graphics to our production, taught magazine show storytelling with ENG (electronic news gathering) equipment, fought hard for resources, and wrote the book on how to produce a live television show with a flexible, living format.

This is important for me to state, because those who view Pat Robertson as a cult leader or snake oil salesman don't understand the reality. *The 700 Club* staff and CBN News were filled with smart and intelligent people very capable of thinking for ourselves. We all knew what was going on and felt it was our duty to get onboard the revolutionary thinking of our evangelical leader. There is simply no way that Pat alone could have accomplished what he did without our ability to think for ourselves and add to the revolution. Chief of all the attributes present among the staff during these years was imagination and creativity. It's not a stretch to say with certainty that our execution of Pat's vision is what made everything possible. History will judge Pat Robertson, for it always looks to the leader, but my stamp—and the stamps of a great many others—are all over the pulpit we gave him.

Further evidence of Pat's early political ambitions came in a September 1984 Gallup research report done for us on the matter of the separation of church and state. Gallup's opening paragraph in the report revealed a doorway of ignorance that could be exploited:

In assessing the results of this survey, it should be borne in
mind that only slightly more than half of Americans (55%)
correctly identify the First Amendment. Furthermore,
more than four in 10 (45%) mistakenly believe that the
statement—"The State shall be separate from the Church,
and the Church from the School"—is found in the U.S.
Constitution.

The latter statement came from the 1977 Constitution of the
Union of Soviet Socialist Republics, the USSR. This and other
findings in the study revealed a great need for education, and that
helped energize us to move forward. We found that the separation of church and state was an important matter for Americans,
and the study showed they felt a strong connection with Ronald
Reagan and his views on the subject. All of this was ammunition
we could use in our efforts to bring the message of salvation to the
masses by any means at our disposal.

The *Saturday Evening Post* article hit the streets in March,
and reaction began popping up here and there, including within
the ministry. A month earlier—and unbeknownst to most of the
staff—Pat had purchased a BAC One-Eleven private jet formerly
owned by singer Kenny Rogers. It had been renumbered NB88,
which we later discovered stood for "New Beginnings in 1988."
This purchase and the subsequent use of the jet would become
a key element of the criminal investigation by the IRS into Pat
Robertson's use of ministry funds in the Robertson campaign.

My first flight on the big jet was in August of 1985, when it was
used to transport us to our annual executive retreat at Pat's stately

vacation home at The Homestead resort in Hot Springs, Virginia. It was here that Pat first told us he was running for president.

"God has told me to run for president and that I will win," were his words to us in a memorable session during that trip. In addition to staff, Harald Bredesen was also there, along with a man we had never met, Michael Clifford, who would later go on to become Pat's campaign manager. Pat's expressed belief was that God had called him to run for president as a means of changing and renewing America. While he felt a conflicting reluctance, he told us he had concluded that he should heed the call and be obedient to what he was hearing from the Lord.

Bredesen, one of the men who had held Ronald Reagan's hand as the 1970 prophecy was given regarding Reagan and the White House, was at the spearhead of Evangelical Christianity's foray into influencing the culture. He was vocal in this meeting about his belief that God had told him "Pat will be the next president." There were very few people in Evangelical Christianity who would dare to challenge the words of Harald Bredesen.

Those present said very little except to offer support. I said nothing, but my mind was churning with a thousand thoughts about what the future held for me and, especially, for *The 700 Club*, because I knew that federal equal time laws prohibited a person running for office from being an ongoing television host. While I was excited to be a part of this historic move and eager to offer my sword in the effort, I also knew immediately what it would do to the program and ultimately the ministry.

The 700 Club was a personality-driven television program, and Pat Robertson was the personality. Without him, there could be no *700 Club*. Nobody present at that meeting, with the possible exception of Executive Producer Michael Little, knew that better than me. There could be no turning back, however, for when Pat Robertson made up his mind to do something, it was etched in stone.

1984 and 1985 were remarkable years to lead the behind-the-scenes creative development and strategic execution of *The 700 Club*. We had the resources, the mission, the vision, and the people available to change the world through television, and it was a heady thing. We were not bashful about it either; we publicly stated that this was our goal.

Throughout my time at CBN, we produced some of the greatest promotional announcements (ads) ever for Christian television. Under the direction of Warren Marcus, we regularly sat at the cutting edge of TV promotion, and I remember one spot in particular that brilliantly presented the idea of changing the world. It was called "raindrops," and it began with one simple raindrop, which evolved into a torrential downpour, which evolved into a small stream, then a raging river and finally into the sea. The brilliance of this ad was that it was a metaphor for many different things associated with CBN. It was about giving, of course, but it was also about participating, which was a constant theme of ours: "You have nothing to complain about in life," we all believed, "if you choose not to be involved."

The politicization of *The 700 Club* and Pat's decision to seek the nation's highest office completely split the ministry of CBN. The dissention was palpable and it worsened the relationships I had with those in positions of authority. I doubt that Pat Robertson fully comprehends that division, although the fruit of it was certainly evident when he returned to the program after losing.

I had a pretty good track record of seeing downstream, and I knew what this was all going to mean to me personally. I chose the easy way out, resigned my position, and returned to the world of local television news. Bob Buford, a Texas millionaire and Christian, gave me the job as news director at KLTV-TV, his station in East Texas.

I knew that the program without Pat would flounder and likely fail. I knew that resources would be taken away as funds to the ministry took their inevitable hit while Pat was both away and asking people to help him fund a presidential campaign. I was tired of being a punching bag for ministry executives who—perhaps honestly—felt they had power and control over Pat Robertson's ministry. I did not like the idea of working for them without Pat to serve as a buffer or to give me a martyr-like reason to justify the pummeling. I knew that the longer I stayed, my history with CBN would make it difficult for me to find employment in my chosen field of TV news. And so I left the ministry in the Spring of 1986 never considering the idea that I might return a year later.

Pat Robertson never made it to the White House, of course, but he left an indelible mark on early twenty-first century grassroots politics through his vision to develop a shadow government. Despite aspirations to alter politics from the top-down through his campaign for president in 1988, it has been the bottom-up efforts of ancillary groups like the Freedom Council, the Christian Coalition of America, and many other subsequent organizations that have taken the Republican Party farther and farther to the right. There are thousands of evangelicals today in positions of local level leadership within the Republican Party. These people represent their faith publicly, and in fact, use it to get elected. There is little doubt that the shadow government exists and is operating as intended.

Pastor and author John Fullerton MacArthur, of the internationally syndicated radio program *Grace to You*, puts it well in his four-part series on Christianity and politics when referencing the moral decay in our culture.

> During the past twenty-five years, well-meaning Christians have founded a number of evangelical activist organizations and sunk millions of dollars into them in an effort to use the apparatus of politics—lobbying, legislation, demonstration, and boycott—to counteract the moral decline of American culture. They pour their energy and other resources into efforts to drum up a "Christian" political movement that will fight back against the prevailing anti-Christian culture.
>
> But is that a proper perspective? I believe not. America's moral decline is a spiritual problem, not a political one, and its solution is the gospel, not partisan politics.[13]

The essential problem that the culture has with this today is that the people who are presenting a "Christian" view in their politics simply do not have the intellectual capacity of a man like the Pat Robertson I knew. And it's not even close. Whether it's right-wing superstar commentators like Rush Limbaugh, Sean Hannity, and Bill O'Reilly, or activists and candidates for the GOP, those who attempt to insert an evangelical perspective into their political views, they all simply come up short in both their understanding and their ability to articulate a "Biblical perspective." Pat says some remarkably insensitive and indefensible things today on *The 700 Club*, and I'm not here to defend the program today. Suffice it to say that his current followers have likely become even more narrow and insensitive as a result.

Consequently, these people tend to come off as clumsy, radical, and dangerous, and their actions often defy even an ounce of reason. I have been a professional observer of life in the US for forty-five years, and the degree to which fundamentalist Christianity dominates people of lesser intelligence and education is one of the most underreported cultural shifts of modern times. The faith seems able to override sense as poor Southerners vote with the Republican Party, which has little or no regard for their status whatsoever. Religion, as a result, can influence people to vote against their own best interests in the name of social issues that aren't really under the authority of the church in the first place. Or perhaps it's more the fear that God will punish them if they don't that drives their actions. Regardless, such contrarian decision-making is found in those who can't or don't really take the time to study or learn to think for themselves, and it's truly as breathtaking as it is heartbreaking.

This is the real weakness and danger of Pat's shadow government, and the evidence is in real world examples. No elected official since this process began better illustrates the issue than Sarah Palin, the former governor of Alaska and vice presidential running mate of Senator John McCain in 2008. The details are well known, but readers need to understand that before Sarah Palin ran for anything, she was an outspoken charismatic, Evangelical Christian who believed in the "gifts of the Spirit" as practiced by many other fundamentalist believers. She spoke the language and knew how to communicate on the edge between faith and politics. Her faith is undeniable and her charisma unmistakable.

Palin was a beauty queen and studied communications in college. Her dream was to be on television, which began in the news business. In my many years in local TV news, I met hundreds of Sarah Palins and never hired any of them. The "be on TV" motivation has ruined the industry, because such people will work for peanuts and produce a product that is a mile wide and an inch deep. In most communications schools across the country today, young people are learning about things such as "how to be on TV" instead of studying the more pertinent things of life, like history, political science, or even English.

In the 2013 three-volume work *Evangelical Christians and Popular Culture: Pop Goes the Gospel*, a series of essays from contemporary authors edited by Robert H. Woods, writer Kevin Healey penned "Constructions of Evangelicalism in Media Coverage of Sarah Palin":

Palin credits Muthee's (Thomas Muthee, bishop of the Word of Faith church in Kiambu, Kenya) "bold" prayer for her success: "And he's praying not, Oh, Lord, if it be your will, may she become governor. No, he just prayed for it. He said, Lord, make a way and let her do this next step. And that's exactly what happened." Such comments shed doubt on the claim that her "task from God" and "pipeline" prayers had been mischaracterized. Indeed, Palin's references to "prayer warriors"—in an interview with (James) Dobson and in her book—are consistent with the views of evangelical groups that advocate aggressive forms of strategic prayer. Drawing from scriptural passages, these groups' leaders have launched controversial campaigns targeting specific ethnic groups, geographic areas, and "strategic towns."[14]

In the minds of many Christians, strategic prayer of this sort is a bridge over the canyon of disbelief, for if God is clearing the way, there's less need to study or do the work for yourself. It is assumed that forces in "the Heavenlies" are at work, so when certain questions are raised, they can be a real stumbling block for those incapable of answering. Questions, for example about qualifications and extreme views on social issues, can seem silly and even shocking to believers, who "know" that God can and will cover any perceived shortcomings.

Sarah Palin was a fan of *The 700 Club* and learned the many phrases and tactics that eventually put her in the Wasilla City Council, the mayor's office, and on to the governor's office in Juneau, Alaska. At every step, she brought along issues like abortion, gun control, term limits, and others that resonated with conservative Christians and, more importantly, Republicans. They had nothing to do with local government, but she was very effective, and her charisma was a weapon she knew she could count on.

John McCain's astonishing choice of Ms. Palin as his running mate in 2008 blew up in his face when CBS anchor Katie Couric interviewed Palin. The governor stumbled badly and came off as intellectually wanting. I wasn't with Pat Robertson when all of this went down, but I would bet good money that he was disappointed. She seemed to fit every right wing criteria except one—she was, as we used to say in East Texas, dumber than a bucket of hair.

Fast-forward to today, and you'll find this lingering ignorance at every level, and the sad thing to me is that only a comic, satirical television program like *The Daily Show* is willing to talk about it. Evangelicals are now so connected and important to the Republican Party that those wishing political office within the GOP, including Donald Trump, must cater to their every wish. It makes it very difficult to judge the character of Republican candidates outside the circle of faith.

What had started as a sincere attempt to arm Christians with the tools of government has turned into a celebration of fools who seem to believe that their religious convictions qualify as a trait of good character and that these convictions make amends for intellectual deficiencies. This is what happens when religion and politics cross paths, especially with Evangelical Christians, where faith bridges any gap in logic and reasoning.

I was a part of this in the early and mid 1980s, and my warning to readers today is to beware of the presumed safety of the group. God wants us to think or He wouldn't have given us brains, and that means learning to think for ourselves. What good is the sacrifice of Jesus, if the grace that came with it is insufficient for our minds and takes us back to the time of hierarchical intercessors? Faith, I've learned the hard way, is vastly more about how we behave—doing what we're supposed to be doing as human beings—than what we believe.

Study and examine everything the group says before signing on, for hierarchies—as I will posit later—always exist for the benefit of those at the top, and faith, in one form or another, is always the tie that binds.

Five

Running for President, 1987–1988

> *"God has told me to run for President and that I will win."*
>
> —Pat Robertson

I was sitting at my desk as news director of KLTV-TV in Tyler, Texas on a Friday in late February 1987 when the telephone rang. Barbara Johnson, Pat Robertson's executive assistant, asked me if I would hold for Pat. I was pretty amazed at that moment and couldn't image why Pat wanted to speak with me. It was my first contact with anybody at CBN since I had left the previous spring, and Pat wouldn't call just to say hello.

"Well, hello there, brother," Pat said to me.

"How are you, sir," I responded.

"I want to ask you two questions," he said. "Can you come to a meeting at my house tomorrow, and would you ever consider coming back here to help me with *The 700 Club?*"

I was stunned and had trouble believing what I had just heard. "Well, I suppose the answer to both would be yes," I said after a few very uncomfortable moments. The first thing that popped into my head was the thought that my wife was miserable in Tyler and how happy she would be if we went back to Virginia Beach.

"It'll take some doing to get me there tomorrow," I said to Pat, "but if you can make the arrangements, I'll be there. What's the meeting about?"

"Good," he said, "I'll see you tomorrow. We're having some difficult discussions about the program, and I think your input would be very useful. We'll have lunch on Sunday and talk about the future."

"Fair enough," I said. "Will anybody know I'm coming?"

"No, brother, and I'd like to keep it that way for now."

Barbara came back on the phone and said she would search travel, make a hotel reservation, and get back to me. I was two hours from Dallas/Fort Worth Airport, so we agreed that I'd fly up first thing Saturday morning. The meeting was scheduled for that afternoon.

I didn't tell anybody at the station that I was going out of town for the weekend, but my wife was delighted. She hadn't shared my desire to return to the stability of local television when I had made the decision to leave CBN in the first place. She also hated the culture and the people of East Texas and longed to return to the beach, and this made it very difficult for me to say anything but yes to Pat's invitation.

CBN hadn't changed much in the year I'd been gone. But as the taxi pulled into the front entrance, it certainly felt different.

Perhaps it was just me. I remember it was cold and snowy. We drove around behind the main facility and outbuildings of CBN University and pulled up in front of Pat's mansion. I was a ball of nerves, because I didn't really know what to expect or what was happening. Mostly, I was already thinking downstream and trying to rationalize a decision to return to what had already been a ministry divided over Pat's decision to run for president. Little did I realize the snake pit it had actually become, nor was I fully prepared for what really was ahead.

I made my entry and sat in the back of the meeting. Pat told the group that he had asked me to attend, because he wanted my advice on the matters being discussed. Eyes popped open as people saw me, and I listened as a heated debate about *The 700 Club* was underway. Knowing that Pat was leaving the show, the producers wanted to change the whole approach of the program, from a TV news magazine to a thematic talk show. This, they reasoned, would better suit the host or hosts that would replace Pat, perhaps for many years as he ran the government. It was good thinking and a good strategy, but I knew that Pat would never, ever go for such a change.

For one, while he behaved every bit like he would win the presidency, he was smart, pragmatic, and political enough to know that he might not. Secondly, there were many executives—and donors—who felt his position as media leader of a Christian movement was actually more important than the presidency. Thirdly, and perhaps most importantly, *The 700 Club* had come a long, long way from its roots as a talk show, and there was just no way Pat would allow it to go back. In his mind, I'm sure, he was happy

to let people play with talk shows, but not *The 700 Club*, because
the program was far more than just a television program that could
be replaced by another. It was the heart and soul of a multi-mil-
lion dollar effort to change the world, and that was really quite
sacred. Tampering with its fabric would be similar to soiling holy
ground. That may seem absurd to some, but this is the context
within which the ministry of CBN was considered at the highest
levels of the faithful.

There was also discussion at the meeting about how funds were
slipping, and it was all mixed together to create an atmosphere of
fear and trembling. I picked up on this immediately, and it further
prompted my own feelings of trepidation about ever coming back.

The meeting broke up without resolution. People said to my
face that it was good to see me and wished me well. Pat and I made
arrangements for lunch the next day, and I was offered a ride to my
hotel, which I accepted.

That night, I went through everything I'd just heard. I had
to be able to answer Pat's question of what I would do if brought
back. My mind raced, and I think I'd already accepted that I
would be returning. I knew Pat Robertson like few others, and
while others have their opinions based on their experiences, Pat
and I communicated non-verbally in ways that I'm still unable to
explain. Mostly, I knew his television program and everything he
was hoping to create with it, without exception. I had come into
the ministry with a television news background and as a rookie
Christian, and while there are church leaders who would suggest
this was a violation of scripture, I always felt it gave me an advantage over others, because I wasn't completely washed in the water

of the Christian way of doing things. I couldn't and wouldn't succumb to such, because I was on a serious mission with the host of the program and rejected the naïveté necessary to march in lock step without question.

This also made me dangerous to those who did so march, because my head went in both directions during important meetings. It gave me a boldness to confront and to offend, if necessary, because I knew exactly what we were doing in bending the rules of "this is how you do it." In boardroom meetings, Pat would often make a creative suggestion and immediately look in my direction, because he *knew* he would get the truth from me, while others simply nodded in agreement. He'd laugh his nervous laugh if I disagreed with something and then announce to the group, "Well, Mr. Heaton doesn't think so much of it." I was utterly unafraid of him on the surface, because I tried to practice the truth of holding my place when the anger of the ruler arose. Pat's bite could be pretty awful. He was a powerful presence with charisma that radiated in every direction. He was also incredibly intelligent and could win any argument.

We would often spar in the dressing room, and I recall one disagreement about the beauty of the Mona Lisa. I thought she was a pretty ugly woman, but Pat insisted her beauty was objective and without question, because the painting was a masterpiece. I reminded him that opinions about art are highly subjective, and I'll never forget his response: "Well, it may be subjective, but I am the subject!" He won with that.

I doubt anyone at CBN had more discussions on strategy with Pat than I did. Nearly every conversation had strategy and tactics at the core, for the mission itself was highly strategic. Nothing was left to chance that could be nailed down strategically. This was CBN. This was Pat Robertson. This was *The 700 Club.*

There were similarities to television news in general, too. The objective was strategic—to grow audience—not to merely serve the information needs of the public. At CBN we were ministering the salvation of Jesus to people across the globe, but strategically we were trying very hard to change that world in order to save it. Yes, we were ministers of the faith, but we were also a highly effective political machine, and our strategy was to link the two in such a way as to produce results. We didn't just point out problems; we wanted also to empower people through solutions that they could support, most of which were via the ballot box or storming Washington and our representatives by telephone with opinions.

Our lunch was nice. We had a private table at a hotel restaurant and talked about things like his wish to get me back on the tennis court. He could never beat me, but that didn't keep him from trying. I think he liked the idea that I wouldn't "let" him win.

After lunch was cleared away, he asked, "What would it take for you to come back and help me, Terry?"

That was a very heady moment for me, so I responded that given the nature of the difficulties ahead for him and the ministry, money wasn't a real consideration for coming back, but that authority would definitely be. Absent the authority to steer the course, the responsibility would crush anybody. I didn't want anyone in my way whatsoever. If he was going to direct me in taking the program to a place that he and his ministry could live with, I would need the authority to direct others who were reticent, regardless of their reasoning. This was the only absolute must that I insisted on, for the job would've been untenable without it. Based on his assurances that it would be so, I agreed to return to CBN as executive producer of *The 700 Club* with responsibilities that included fundraising and, finally, CBN News.

I should have known that he would be unable later to fulfill this promise, but the red flag was covered up by my ego and the need to please my wife. The result was I walked right into a trap.

Michael Little had been my "boss" during my previous tenure at CBN. At the time, he was executive producer and I was senior producer. We often had conflicts over matters of running the program. I knew what Pat wanted, but it was Michael's job to make sure those "wants" were in line with the business of running the ministry. There was a budget, after all, and an accounting process that demanded attention. It is in this area more than any other that there existed a grave disconnect within the ministry. On the one hand, there was a group of executives who lived by an organizational chart that had no basis in reality, for CBN was, at best, a chaotic cult of personality in which there was no organizational chart. There was Pat, and there was everybody else.

It was the dream of order in the minds of other executives that created a system within which Pat could be managed, at least in their minds. There was no managing Pat Robertson, however, and the mere suggestion of it was folly gone to seed. The energy wasted in this effort was truly remarkable. It was like trying to put handles on a slippery greased pig, and those who couldn't see that relentlessly frustrated me. In the end, it was all about the mission, and it was the only thing that truly mattered. Trying to control the entrepreneurial vision of its genius founder through the systems and processes of modern business was an unnecessary governor for an engine that could run at unprecedented speeds.

Technically I replaced Mr. Little as executive producer, but in reality I didn't. Michael was now president, so I was technically still beneath him. Nothing was different according to the organizational chart. I reported to Tim Robertson, Pat's son, so the authority that I had sought was mostly an illusion, and it was so from the beginning. I operated with one set of beliefs, while the rest of the "business" functioned under another. I needed Pat to referee, but he simply wasn't there.

There are those who will judge me arrogant for assuming I could push my way into a position of authority above them and their experience, but remember, I trusted Pat Robertson to be a man of his word. He knew exactly what I was talking about in terms of expectations, but as much as he needed me, he also needed the structure of CBN to remain intact and functioning. Sadly, it was a zero sum quagmire that I could not overcome. Nevertheless, I gave it my best shot.

Every top line producer of a television program has enemies in the ranks. I was no fool in that regard, and besides, I accepted years earlier that being the buffer between Pat Robertson and others at the ministry was a lose-lose proposition. It is why I had constant stomach and bowel problems, because it could be like working inside a running washing machine. I had to swallow pain like few could know, because Pat Robertson was trying to change the world, and I was there to help him. Period.

Few people actually change the world, because it's hard. The opportunity to participate in such was incredibly exciting to me, but it would've been so much easier if there weren't hundreds of others at the ministry insisting we should just be preaching Jesus. Anybody could do that, and I can say with great certainty that Pat had no greater ally in his mission than Terry Heaton. I was completely loyal to the task, and I had the experience and skills to implement what was necessary to that end. It could be, however, a terribly lonely place, and in the end, it became clear that the task was impossible.

While he was admired and respected at all levels of the ministry, Pat Robertson was also the enemy of management. This is what happens when those who count the beans encounter a leader who wants and needs to work outside the governors of process and system. I have seen it in other jobs, and it's a sad commentary on Western culture, for there is a deep difference between managers and leaders. Leaders appreciate that in every situation a little chaos may be necessary, but managers insist that planning and processes should be the final word. This conflict was evident to me, and unfortunately, somebody had to take the wants and needs of the leader and fit those square pegs into the round holes of CBN management.

This conflict got worse with every day that passed after I returned, and one big reason was that contributions fell off a cliff in the wake of Oral Roberts' pronouncement during his January 1987 telethon that unless he raised $8 million over the next couple of months, God would "take him home," a Christian euphemism for ending his life. This preposterous and self-centered statement gave reporters in Tulsa the ammunition they needed to open the doors of the "faith healer's" ministry, and soon coverage spread nationwide and beyond.

At nearly the same time, Jim Bakker fell from grace at his PTL (Praise The Lord) ministry in Charlotte, North Carolina. The discovery of his tryst with Jessica Hahn and the subsequent cover-up broke a dam of pent-up mistrust of televangelists in the press, and what followed was a broad brush with which they painted every television ministry, including the one founded by the guy now in the White House. The Bakker debacle occurred on March 19, 1987, just weeks before my return to CBN. The ugly spotlight was on everyone, as the ghost of Sinclair Lewis's Elmer Gantry visited all levels of society, including those we had worked so hard to recruit since the beginning of the 1980s. It is impossible to overstate how badly these events impacted Christian ministries, and especially evangelicals on TV, including the ministry of Pat Robertson.

The result was that I returned in early April and walked right into a reduction in force that ultimately cost over 500 people their jobs, including forty-three percent of my staff. Management made the decision to adjust the payroll and staffing in such a way that would assume a permanency to the new contribution levels rather than ride out the storm in the belief that the money would come back. It is hard to argue with this decision, although it hardly reflected faith in anything other than their ability to manage a crisis. That's easy for me to say today, I suppose, but there was a spirit of dread that hung over the ministry in those days that influenced every corner of the campus. It was striking to observe a group of people who alleged faith and trust in an Almighty God give in to fear in the middle of a crisis.

In press reports in the wake of the layoffs, Pat Robertson laid the blame directly at the feet of Jim Bakker and Oral Roberts. The following is from an article in the *Philadelphia Inquirer*:

> "We have probably the finest forecasting and budgeting processes in the evangelical world, but it is impossible to forecast an atomic explosion," Robertson said on his television program, *The 700 Club*. "We had nothing to do with any of it."
>
> He said the PTL scandal and the Rev. Oral Roberts' "life-or-death" appeal for money had cost Robertson's Christian Broadcasting Network $12 million in contributions so far and probably would drain $28 million by the end of the year.
>
> "In the history of American Christianity, we have never seen anything like this," said Robertson, who is considering a run for Republican presidential nomination. "That scandal has hit the evangelical world like a bombshell."[15]

This businesslike action by the ministry caused a monumental problem for me as Pat Robertson's executive producer, for in reality I had virtually none of the authority I was promised during that lunch with Pat. Despite all the talk of "faith," we exhibited the opposite in a time of crisis, and I don't believe it reflected well on us, as a ministry, as to our calling, or as those "men with knowledge of the times." We were hypocrites, and it was just beginning.

Was Pat Robertson's calling to run for president "of God" or not? The evidence suggests not, but it hasn't all been collected just yet. History will have its say. The more important matter to me is whether the man's ministry was behind the calling or not. Behavior always trumps proclamations of faith, and the behavior of the executive team and the board of directors in the wake of Pat's actual candidacy was generally not in line with what we had declared through our mission, our teachings, and our ministry.

As we say and believe in Alcoholics Anonymous, "...either God is everything or else He is nothing. God either is, or He isn't. What was our choice to be?" Corporate CBN made the decision, and the faithful had no choice but to follow its lead.

And it certainly didn't make my job any easier in coming back, for I was by now the master of a clearly sinking ship. I was trapped. I knew it. And there was nothing I could do except to pray for guidance and plunge myself deeply into the task at hand.

The public spotlight was on every ministry, and murmuring and fear covered the CBN campus in ways that were terribly unhealthy. One of the first events after I got back was concern expressed by certain contributors and subsequently managers over the behavior of co-host Danuta Soderman's husband, Kai Soderman. I was told that he was suspected of approaching major donors with his own big money development projects, which was definitely not all right with those who oversaw fundraising for CBN. It reflected badly on Danuta, who was having an internal crisis of her own at the time. She described it herself in her book *Chiseled: A Memoir of Identity, Duplicity, and Divine Wine*:

I needed a break during Pat's campaign. I felt useless, a fixture on a political show pieced together at the last minute on Robertson's whims. For months, Pat disregarded the preparations of the show's producers, running into the studio at the last minute, haranguing the audience with thirty-minute off-the-cuff speeches, while Ben and I sat silently nodding and smiling, trying to look interested.

When I expressed my concerns, Terry understood. "I know it's frustrating, Danuta. I'm the one tossing out schedules and rearranging formats. I don't even know what the show is, and I'm the producer." He shrugged his shoulders back and readjusted his tie.

I told Terry that I believed my tenure at CBN had run its course and that Kai and I were thinking of moving back to California. He looked alarmed. "Don't make any hasty plans," he said. "All you need is some time off. You're tired. Take a break, go to the beach. You'll feel better when you get back. But promise me you won't make any sudden decisions."

With the promise made, Kai and I took a week off to rest and relax and to evaluate my role at CBN."[16]

I looked alarmed to Danuta, because I was terribly alarmed. Danuta was a professional journalist before she became a Christian, and she was my confidante and friend. We were kindred spirits and shared many of the same concerns about the line between right and wrong in the dissemination of information. While CBN in many ways pioneered point-of-view journalism, pioneers are the people in history who end up with arrows in their backs, and that metaphor was certainly evident at the ministry. I had the wounds to prove it and so did Danuta.

I went to Pat, Tim, Michael Little, and Bob Slosser and expressed my concern that Danuta was a key part of my plans for after Pat went on the campaign, and that letting her walk away would be a serious mistake.

That's why I found myself in Naples, Florida a few days later with Harald Bredesen, Danuta's spiritual "father." Our mission was simple: do what was necessary to minister to Danuta and Kai and keep her as a vital personality in the shaping of a program without Pat. It turned out to be a difficult task, but after three days, she agreed to return with assurances that I would have her back.

In the light of history, it's easy to say that perhaps my plan wasn't the best plan for Danuta, because while I was gone, the decision had been made to remove her as co-host of *The 700 Club*. The only person who could make such a decision was Pat Robertson, and I was never given an explanation about how this was in the best interests of the program or the ministry. As Danuta describes it in *Chiseled*, it was a decision based on politics and the potential for her to be an embarrassment (real or imagined) to Pat's campaign. The only thing I was ever told was that it was all about her husband's exploitation of her position to gain access to deep pockets. I don't know any deeper truth, but regardless of the reason, the decision broke my heart. I knew how to make good television, and Danuta was a pro's pro. I needed her, and badly.

It was a shame on everybody involved to cut her loose and in such a way as to deny her the opportunity to say goodbye on the air or give her followers an explanation as to why. It was unprofessional. It was personal. It was awful. As far as the show was concerned, she simply disappeared, and there's no way I can justify any of it.

Danuta wrote in her book that I informed her of the decision in the parking lot of CBN and how it was poorly handled. I do not disagree. It was my duty as executive producer to deliver the news, but my orders came with instructions to not let a minute pass without giving her notice. That forced me to grab her before she left, because once the decision had been made, she was not welcome on the set of *The 700 Club.* Top management did not want any ugliness in either the studio or the dressing rooms the following morning, even though I tried to assure Pat that this would be highly unlikely given Danuta's experience as a professional television host. And so, in one of the more miserable duties I ever had to fulfill in my life as a manager, I fired Danuta in that parking lot.

Danuta describes this gathering well and completely in her book, and there's no need for me to echo her statements. It was as unpleasant for me as it was for her, but nobody getting fired cares about such, nor are they expected to. It's very hard to fire people you love, but it's even harder to be on the receiving end. And I dearly loved Danuta Soderman. She was a trouper's trouper and did not deserve to end her service at CBN the way she did. I was ashamed of myself and for the ministry, and the whole mess impacted me deeply as a person.

....

One of the CBN News reporters, Kathy Bullock, had long impressed me with her natural presence on camera and her intelligence as a correspondent. In the vernacular of TV consultants, Kathy "got past the glass" on TV, meaning she had the unique ability to grab attention beyond the screen by having the looks and personality to really communicate. She was young, but she was comfortable in the co-host chair and did a wonderful job filling in after Danuta was canned. My initial inclination was to press for her to become the new co-host, but Pat and those who nodded their heads in lockstep with every opinion he expressed torpedoed the idea. Pat felt she was too young and inexperienced, although that was neither my view nor the view of others on my staff.

I first called Terry Meeuwsen, an old friend from my news days in Milwaukee. Terry was a former Miss America and a gifted on-air host. She had filled in occasionally and was a natural new co-host for *The 700 Club*. Unfortunately, family and work made her moving to Virginia Beach impossible at the time, although she did become co-host many years later.

My next thought was to contact Susan Howard, one of the stars of the hit TV show *Dallas*. I had met her when we had taken *The 700 Club* to California several years earlier, and I thought she would bring along new viewers and followers. I called in every mark I had with people in Hollywood and in the ministry, and we eventually convinced her to come aboard. This was a very big deal, because she was an A-List Hollywood celebrity.

While Susan brought with her certain Hollywood backstage expectations, she was truly wonderful as co-host of the program. Her presence on the set lifted the show at a time when it really needed lifting. She was dynamic and her face lit up the screen, adding a certain kind of credibility to a TV ministry program that was under deep public scrutiny. She was kind and compassionate, and the employees of CBN loved her. Pat and Ben worked well with her, and soon Danuta's loss seemed like water under the bridge to most people. I knew better, however, because I doubted the permanence of Susan's efforts. She was a California gal and an actress. Her husband came with her, and his only concern, justifiably, was Susan and her career. Despite my doubts, I had hired her anyway, because the program badly needed a breath of fresh air, and Susan was certainly that.

Pat Robertson grew more political on the program as the days, weeks, and months passed. When he was away, we were able to occasionally run segments titled "Pat Robertson's Perspective" that were shot on a different, more authoritatively designed set. I had proposed in 1984 that we convert the last half-hour of the ninety-minute *700 Club* to a stand-alone half-hour program of the same name. I thought we might be able to syndicate it separately from *The 700 Club* and that it might relieve our show from the encroachment of political segments. We built the set to create a pilot, but the whole thing was snubbed. We later used it to create segments, so that Pat could still appear to be on the show, even though he was on the "unofficial" campaign.

In both 1986, prior to my leaving, and 1987, there were new faces that were occasionally in Pat's dressing room and around the set of the program, mostly connected with Pat's campaign, and lines began to get blurred. Jerry Curry, one of Pat's closest advisors, sent me a memo in April of 1986:

> I suppose this is somewhat presumptuous, but I keep running into Reagan officials whom Pat might want to select for key jobs in a Robertson Administration, should the need ever arise. It occurs to me that one way for Pat to get acquainted with these folks would be to interview them on *The 700 Club*. So, consider this Memo Number One in the great search for new talent. Unless you have a problem with me reducing this to writing, I will run these names by you on a periodic basis.

He then recommended Alan E. Sears, staff director of the Meese Commission on pornography at the Justice Department—"Alan is the type of person we would want to select for a top job at the Justice Department, if not the top job itself"; Ralph Stanley, head of the Urban Mass Transportation Administration—"He would make an outstanding Secretary of Transportation"; and Dave Swoap, architect of the Reagan welfare program in California. Curry wanted him for Secretary of Health and Human Services and added, "Dave, who is about 45, brings the same kind of intellectual quality to his work that you and Pat bring to yours."

> And, for the record, let's not forget Ollie North at the National Security Council. Three more years in that job and he ought to be ready to take [John] Poindexter's place [Reagan's National Security Advisor].
> Now, how do we get these guys on *The 700 Club*?

The point is that we regularly crossed the line of what most would consider ethical and what the IRS would deem illegal according to the laws that governed 501(c)(3) tax-exempt organizations. I tried wherever possible to keep things in check, but the truth is I was complicit with Pat and his election team in pushing the envelope even over the line. I felt it was something that I could manage, although that line was always a moving target. Remember, we were trying to change the world for the better, and what did it matter as long as God was on our side? I struggled internally, but I had made the decision to come back to CBN, and I knew what Pat wanted and needed. It added to my stress, of course, but I was willing to go there for the chance to be a part of history. Danuta also experienced this same feeling of being over the ethical line and expressed it succinctly in her book:

> My mere presence on the set of *The 700 Club* made me an accessory to a progressively wilder and more extreme view of Christianity. Worse, I was helping leverage a campaign to make Pat the most powerful man in the world. I tried justifying my position with the argument that politics and faith are intertwined; both require judgments based on morality. But deep down inside, I was still a journalist insisting on documentation.[17]

When we produced live reports from the scene of certain campaign stops, it was always my idea to do so. Let's face it, *The 700 Club* is a personality-driven television show, and Pat Robertson was the personality. Remove him from the program, and you remove its edge, and that was something I felt certain that I had to protect. And so my decisions always advanced the campaign and gave Pat the platform he needed to speak to and with his supporters around the country. It was "free," if you will, but it was questionable both ethically and legally. We were publicly presenting ourselves as a news organization, and many of us suspected that this was nothing more than wishful thinking.

The IRS began investigating CBN and the Freedom Council, a 501(c)(4) organization supported by the ministry, in the early fall of 1986, just after Pat had made his initial announcement about seeking the presidency if three million citizens would sign a petition of support. The timing of this criminal investigation by a federal agency is important to understand as it pertains to the whole business of Pat running for president. After all, his chief opponent during the campaign was George H. W. Bush, the sitting vice president.

Portions of my deposition with the IRS Criminal Investigative Division are published later in this book, but the point is it cast a pall over the entire ministry and was constantly a subject of discussion as I went about my job day in and day out. Let me say again that Pat's running for president was not fully endorsed by the management team at CBN, and I had to deal with the fallout from certain guests or segments we did. I was always working for two masters at the ministry, and they were very often not on the same page.

In my dealings with everyone, I had no choice but to let my actions reflect a belief that Pat would win the election. Not only was I a leader at CBN, but, in many ways, I was Pat's right-hand man as it pertained to the primary instrument of CBN, *The 700 Club*. I would not have come back in 1987 had I not believed in what we were doing. Every decision I made carried that as a core justification, and it didn't matter if I was eventually proved right or wrong. The issue was what to do today, and that meant becoming a rower in Pat's boat. To live in the future, especially one governed by fear was not the right choice for anyone in my position.

I often led worship at prayer meetings with the ministry. In the last prayer meeting before Pat began an extended period of campaigning, I played "Hail to the Chief" on my guitar as he left the room with a thousand people silent. It got his attention, and he smiled. It was my way of wishing him Godspeed on the journey.

We soldiered on in Pat's absence, occasionally using pre-taped segments of "Pat's Perspective" to fill the gap, but things outside our control made the task of delivering a television program without Pat Robertson difficult, at best.

On many occasions, I was able to convince Charles Colson, one of the Watergate co-conspirators and subsequent founder of Prison Fellowship, to either co-host the program in Pat's absence or tape segments we could use later. Chuck became a dear friend, and the work we did together on *The 700 Club* was among some of my best. He was a supporter of Pat's efforts and brought a similar, authoritative and conservative view of public policy and analysis of current events. He was philosophically a pragmatist and didn't believe in the charismata, or "gifts" of the Holy Spirit in the practice of Christianity and especially at CBN. He was a highly intelligent observer of current events, however, and quite comfortable in Pat's chair. He could easily handle the "father figure" role necessary in the on-air chemistry of the program.

He once told me of being approached by Dallas televangelist Robert Tilton in Texas and advised to "embrace" speaking in tongues and proclaiming the gifts of the spirit. Tilton's reasoning? "That's where the money is." Colson smiled when he told me that, and I knew what he meant. Money was the curse of televangelism in the 1980s, and Chuck Colson wanted nothing to do with it.

In one of his letters to me many years later, he wrote, "You should know that after you left CBN, I was never invited back again." He always thanked me for the opportunities he was given to be of service, and it's a shame he was never considered good enough to bring on as a replacement in Pat's absence.

By January of 1988, the ministry of CBN was in deep trouble financially. CBN was the home of gifted marketers and fundraising development specialists who lived and died by statistics, and the stats by that time were dreadful, especially those showing direct ministry between CBN telephone counselors and callers. We measured everything from salvation prayers to ministering to people contemplating suicide. Comparing ministry stats from January of 1988 with January of 1987 was revealing:

Specific Ministry	1987	1988	% Variation
Calls	685,724	346,088	−49
Salvations	34,130	17,850	−47
Prayer Requests	396,176	243,777	−38
Answers to Prayer	9,763	4,901	−49
Holy Spirit Baps	10,672	9,031	−15
Family Counsel	114,902	81,496	−29
Drugs	12,152	8,479	−30
Alcohol	15,525	7,753	−50
Sexual Deviates	6,122	3,482	−43
Suicides	1,331	908	−31

This drop of nearly half was primarily the result of the televange-list scandals, and the media suggested that Pat Robertson's cam-paign for president was in the same category. It placed the entire ministry in jeopardy and was impossible to overcome given the circumstances.

Nevertheless, I tried. We held a planning retreat at The Homestead in Hot Springs and numerous internal meetings, research, and trials. I brought in the top TV consulting company Audience Research & Development (AR&D), from my back-ground in the news business, which I later learned didn't sit well with some. Ben and Susan were still onboard, to which I wanted to add Chuck Colson. That was rejected, and so I turned to two people already at the ministry, Scott Ross, a minister to the music industry with the ability to recruit a younger audience, and Bob Slosser, a long-time ministry leader as CEO, president of Regent University, senior editor of CBN News, and a former *New York Times* assistant editor. While soft-spoken, Bob had the credentials and the chops to function as commentator on current events. It had seemed to me that this team—with the proper support—could carry on the ministry and mission of *The 700 Club* until Pat's cam-paign was over, whether he won or not.

This was not to be the case, however, and the event that led up to the final decision about who would host *The 700 Club* was one of the ugliest and most personally devastating experiences of my life.

The date was January 31, 1988, the final Sunday of the final CBN telethon before Pat left the show. Telethons were a lot of work, and this one was no exception. We went live in both the

morning and in the evening for two straight weeks. The money
raised in January in the form of memberships sold and gifts was a
significant part of the annual budget for the ministry. Telethons
were super important, and Pat was often as tense off the air as he
was confident and energetic on the air. He could bite like few
people I've ever known, and the demand for excellence was never
higher. For my staff and myself it was often a grueling time of
long hours in a tense and stressful atmosphere. Of course, all was
forgiven when we were done, because the telethons were usually
very successful.

But this was January of 1988, and the need to raise money was
even greater than it had been in past years.

One of the rules we had was that all employees were required
to work the phones at least once during telethons. I usually waited
until the last day, and this was no exception. Working the phones
during a Christian fundraising event was not easy. The volume
of crank, obnoxious, and vulgar calls that are placed to a toll-free
number in such occurrences was truly staggering, so it was necessary when working the phones to prepare. This meant quiet time
and prayer. I was given a reserved seat in the front of the caller
platform, from where I would often comment on the air about
how things were going on the phones, for the next many hours.

I arrived on the campus several hours ahead of schedule to
check in with staff preparations, after which I went directly to
the prayer room above the chapel near the entrance to the broadcast building. This was a remarkable, circular room, with a sweet
spiritual presence throughout. It wasn't so much cloying, as it was
a tangible sign of encouragement, because it felt so right. People

prayed out loud and silently, but the energy in the room was thick, uplifting, and actually quite powerful. I was on my knees and prone on the floor for about two hours, and then I headed for the studio. I was prepared for anything, or so I thought.

I took my seat, and moments before the program went on the air, Dede Robertson, Pat's wife, came walking down the stairs in my direction. Dede was always cold and distant to me, whether she was entertaining at the private Christmas party at her home, helping out at the retreat house in Hot Springs, or on visits to the program. She treated me like one of the help, in the same way that you might imagine a Southern plantation "ma'am" treating the help there.

And here she was at the very beginning of my long shift on the phones heading in my direction. She came up to me and addressed me in front of everyone.

"How *dare* you?" she demanded. "How *dare* you bring in people from Dallas, of all places, to try and tell my girls how to do hair and make-up? How *dare* you!"

The look on her face would have frozen a raging inferno if it hadn't been for the steam rising from her head. I had never seen her so angry, and she was enraged. Her wrath was directed at me for bringing in consultants from AR&D in Dallas to advise us on everything. Obviously, "her girls"—the hair and makeup staff of CBN and *The 700 Club*—had complained to Mrs. Robertson while dolling her up for the telethon, and she wanted to demonstrate her disapproval in such a way as to communicate it clearly.

Before I could respond, my telephone rang. It was somebody telling me to "go fuck myself," and so it went for the entire program. All of my preparation had been ruined, and I sat there helpless as the hours ticked by. It was about to get worse.

When the show finally ended, we were all exhausted and stressed, even though the work was over. Pat, however, had one more subject that he wanted to address with a few others and me: what would we do beginning the next day when he wasn't going to be there? I recall Ben being present, along with Michael Little, Tim Robertson, Bob Slosser, Scott Ross, and perhaps a few others. Susan Howard had left, so it was entirely a meeting of men.

I felt disapproval even before it was announced, and even more so after I shared, once again, my plans for the coming week and beyond.

Pat Robertson could handle just about anything when it came to television, but he was adamant that he would not allow others to potentially raise their own ministry money. This was the issue that was behind the split between Pat and Jim and Tammy Bakker in the early 1970s. The Bakkers had helped him build CBN and *The 700 Club*, but then wanted to be able to raise their own funds for their own ministry on the CBN network. Pat refused. There followed a mysterious fire in the studio that housed the Bakkers' set, and Jim and Tammy moved from Portsmouth, Virginia, to California in furtherance of their own ministry.

Pat was agitated and irritated in the meeting following the telethon, and after rejecting every word that came out of my mouth, he turned to his son and said, "Tim, you're going to have to do this."

Tim Robertson was more like his mother than his father. He was brilliant and a gifted business administrator, but he had very little charisma, no desire to be public, and no experience being on television. His face red, he objected, saying it would be terrible for the ministry if he were to try and replace his father on *The 700 Club*.

Pat would have none of it and said, "Tim, you can do it. I need you to do it. Terry and the staff will help you. It'll be all right."

But everybody in the room knew it wouldn't be, and despite my protests, nobody stood up and argued with Pat Robertson. His issue was money. He didn't want anyone whose name wasn't Robertson at the helm of things on the air. His oldest son, Gordon, who was a chip off the old block in terms of charm, wit, and charisma, wanted nothing to do with the ministry, although that would change many years later.

Meanwhile, Tim just stood there embarrassed and uncomfortable and looked at me. "I guess I'll see you in the morning."

And that was it. I suppose I should have seen it coming, but I didn't and neither did anybody else. It was what it was going to be, and I had no choice but to swallow hard and move on. But my heart was never in it after that day. Tim was beyond awful in those first few appearances, and it looked for every reason to be exactly what it was, a father handing off his ministry to his son, regardless of the outcome. I was beaten down and miserable, and I should have taken responsibility for my life and career and resigned right then. I didn't because I had a family to support, and I needed time to think. I put on a soldier's face and did the best I could with what I had. It would never be enough.

Pat made an appearance every now and then, including on February 9, 1988, the day after he finished ahead of Bush in the Iowa caucuses. I had watched network coverage the night before as Pat got into an on-air confrontation with Tom Brokaw of NBC, who kept referring to him as a televangelist. Pat rightly felt that this was deliberately pejorative, and he went after Brokaw. It wasn't terribly smart, because a candidate will never win against a network anchor.

In the dressing room that morning, I told him I thought he had made a mistake. In my years with Pat, he'd always appreciated my opinion, whether he agreed with it or not. He just liked the idea that I had the strength to tell him what I thought. This time, however, he got angry.

"If I'm the halfback of the football team," he argued, "and the play-by-play announcer calls me the fullback, whose responsibility is that? It's certainly not mine as the player. He was wrong, and I had no choice but tell him so."

We went back and forth for a while but, naturally, I lost the argument. Pat's ability to bring out a metaphor at a moment's notice was one of his true gifts, but it didn't feel very good that morning.

We tried many combinations of hosts with and without Tim in the weeks that followed. Susan Howard went back to California, and it was hard to blame her. She had given us six months, and that was more than enough in her mind, especially given the turbulent nature of things behind the scenes and on the air.

Kathy Bullock and Cindy Glaser filled in for her as we opened yet another search for a female co-host. We had built a new set—one that the local paper said matched *Miami Vice* colors, even though that was never our intention. We wanted contemporary, and pastels were the big thing, whether spawned by *Miami Vice* or not.

Pat had given us instructions that included this Bible verse:

No one tears a patch from a new garment and sews it on an old one. If he does, he will have torn the new garment, and the patch from the new will not match the old. And no one pours new wine into old wineskins. If he does, the new wine will burst the skins, the wine will run out and the wineskins will be ruined. No, new wine must be poured into new wineskins. And no one after drinking old wine wants the new, for he says, "the old is better." (Luke 5:36-39)

I was all for new wine, but I had never planned that the program would completely lose its identity in the process. Ben Kinchlow announced his departure, as things at the ministry worsened. I could hardly blame him. Ben had been second chair on the program for many years, and he was passed over in the name of keeping a Robertson at the helm. I was powerless to stop the slide. The CBN board met the week of March 14, consolidated power with Tim, announced a major restructuring under Tim, and terminated my employment as executive producer of *The 700 Club*.

A report in the *Virginian Pilot* newspaper on March 18 noted the restructuring:

To jump-start CBN's flagship show, *The 700 Club*, the seven-member board also ordered CBN to launch a nationwide search for new on-air talent and a better format for the religious talk show.

"You've heard the old adage, 'Don't give God junk,'" CBN spokesman Benton Miller said. "The board felt *The 700 Club* needed to be more compelling."

Pat and Dede were both board members, and when I asked if Pat had signed off on my firing, Bob Slosser gave me a definite "yes." I don't know if Dede was involved, but it didn't matter anymore. Nothing mattered anymore. I was told that I could stay on with CBN and that they would find another position for me, but I took some time off to think. I still have my notes from that week, as my wife and I tried to figure out our next move. Should we stay or should we go?

Later that year, my former mother-in-law in Manitowoc, Wisconsin, herself a long time viewer and contributor to *The 700 Club*, wrote to Pat to complain about my firing. I have the letter Pat wrote back to her, in which he wrote, "Terry is a wonderful young man. I love him and think very highly of him. I had nothing to do with him leaving CBN—that decision was made before I came back." This was contrary to what I had been told by Mr. Slosser, and I have no idea who is telling the truth.

I was broken in many ways. I put on a good face, and even went to Pat's house after getting a new job in Chattanooga months later. I didn't make an appointment; I simply knocked on the door. I think I went there to confront him, but I instead told him I held nothing against him personally over what had happened in the previous year. We hugged and he prayed for me, and that was that. My spirit was crushed and the heart I had so willingly given to him was broken in two. I fell into a deep funk, and journaled:

> Nobody told me I would be responsible for everything. I didn't come back to be anybody's hero, but did I deserve disrespect? Nobody told me that Danuta would have to

go, that Dede thinks Texans are tasteless, that Jon Simpson
had resigned, that Dottie was leaving, that I couldn't use
Scott Ross, that Sam Walker would be forced on the air
3 months early, that Susan Howard would quit after 6
months, that I would lose almost half my staff, that I would
lose commensurate pre and post production resources, that
Ben would leave, that we would let the IRS dictate edito-
rial content, that Tim would become a permanent co-host,
and that everything would be a committee decision.

I sent Tim a memo dated April 13, 1988:

On March 18, 1988, I was notified by Bob Slosser of the
decision by the CBN Board of Directors to replace me as
Executive Producer of *The 700 Club*. That was followed
by your gracious offer to allow me to remain at CBN in
some other capacity.

I have the greatest respect and admiration for you and the
management team at CBN but, after prayerful consideration,
believe it is the Lord's will for me to move on at this time.

Therefore, I respectfully decline your offer and submit
my resignation, effective April 8, 1988. I harbor no ill will
toward you (or anyone else at CBN) over these events and
look forward to our eternal friendship.

And that was that, which left me with the unanswerable question
of whether my choosing to return a year earlier had been a mistake. I had lost over $70,000 in relocating back to Virginia Beach,

and the pain of the whole experience was overwhelming nearly every day that I tried to help Pat. To be fired by him after all the promises just one year earlier was really hard to take. And then there was the question of missing God's calling or not. It was all too much, and I started drinking heavily, something that would profoundly alter my relationship with the God I loved.

I was given an excellent severance package that included three monthly checks that covered my base salary. For whatever reason, they sent me four checks, and when I got a letter from Tim later acknowledging the error and asking me to send it back, I refused. In my view, it was a bonus for pain and suffering, and my heart hardened further.

Over years of introspection, I gave a great deal of thought to what we had done in those years in the 1980s. We had actually redefined what it meant to be a conservative Republican, and this was no small feat. We altered the balance of power in the GOP by bringing in millions of Christians who were able to look completely past the reality that Republicans represented the wealthy first. This was an amazing accomplishment, but one that has left our culture in a really bad situation, for fundamentalist Christians were a key element of Donald Trump's election. Pat noted this movement in his book *The Plan*, and reading it today sends a chill down my spine as I survey the cultural damage done by this angry mob.

Could it be that the reason for my candidacy has been fulfilled in the activation of tens of thousands of evangelical Christians into government? This campaign taught them that they were citizens with as much right to express their beliefs as any of the strident activists who have been so vocal in support of their own radical agenda at every level of our government. For the first time in recent history, patriotic, pro-family Christians learned the simple techniques of effective party organizing and successful campaigning.[18]

To be clear, it wasn't Pat's campaign that did this; it was *The 700 Club* television program. Before Rush Limbaugh, there was Pat Robertson.

While many of the young and intelligent group we targeted with our message had moved on, the people left accepted everything we taught them, and their belief that Jesus was and is Himself proud of their accomplishments makes it impossible to reason with them. And yet they regularly vote against their own best interests as poorer people largely from the South who could use a helping hand every now and then. But they don't see it that way and believe instead that they are the givers of charity, not ever to be the recipients, for that would violate their faith, even though there isn't a one who can say exactly how. Perhaps it's envy or just wishful thinking that compels them to align themselves with the modern-day Pharisees, when they, in truth, are much more a part of the have-nots. It is much more the parroting of what they've been told, by the televangelists, back then and now beyond, led by people like Pat Robertson, myself, the ministry of CBN, and a gospel message that appeals to the self-centered wants and needs of its followers, the gospel of self.

Six

The IRS vs. Pat Robertson, 1988

The only two things that scare me are God and the IRS.
—Dr. Dre

Federal agencies like the Internal Revenue Service and the Federal Election Commission were very interested in Pat Robertson's campaign for president of the United States, and most of that interest involved money. CBN was a tax-exempt ministry, just like any church. For example, until the IRS changed the rules, we did not pay Social Security taxes, so Pat created individual retirement accounts for each employee through Fidelity Investments. The ministry contributed its Social Security share and our paychecks were "taxed" at the same level as Social Security. The big difference was that the money went into individual interest-bearing accounts that we could access upon retirement. The amount of money in my account, which was only over a period of a few years, was mid five figures.

When someone leading a ministry runs for public office, however, that tax exemption qualifies for close scrutiny, and two federal agencies paid close attention. One, of course, was the IRS. The other was the Federal Election Commission. Somebody has to bring a complaint, an order, or some other notice that something is amiss in order to launch costly investigations, and in the Washington bureaucracy, such calls are quite often politically based. Pat was running for president, the same office that sitting Vice President George H. W. Bush was seeking. It does not take a genius to creatively explore the politics involved here, and while I can't prove anything, the prevailing view in my circle was that Mr. Bush had set it all in motion.

Vice President Bush had the means, the motive, and the opportunity to run a stake through the heart of the Robertson candidacy, and while I'll admit that we broke the tax laws, and by extension, Federal Election Commission rules in the process, the timing of these investigations favored only Mr. Bush. The question of whether there would ever have been an investigation were one of the candidates not the sitting vice president is one that cannot be answered fairly. It is the timing that matters most. Regardless, the weight of these probes impacted daily life at CBN, for we were forced into placing every decision underneath the microscope of threats to our tax exemption. We played defense only, the wind had been taken out of the sails of our offensive efforts.

In August of 1988, Pat Robertson took the podium at the Republican National Convention in the Superdome in New Orleans and addressed attendees about issues that were important to him. He then endorsed George Bush and asked his followers to vote for Mr. Bush. Knowing how Pat really felt about Bush, this had to be both humiliating and agonizing. Granted, it was a political necessity, but I have always felt there was more to it than that.

I had for the most part recovered from the wounds of getting fired by Pat and was working as news director at WDEF-TV in Chattanooga when I received a phone call from the Criminal Investigative Division (CID) of the IRS requesting my presence at a deposition in early September. I was frankly terrified, for I knew my role in the use of ministry monies but I also knew much more. It is important to understand that the IRS is no respecter of persons, and that its long arms can go anywhere. This was a criminal investigation, and as much as I still loved and respected Pat Robertson, I did not want to go to jail for the man, even as unlikely as that was. One cannot appreciate the trepidation that comes when confronted with the full weight of the IRS unless one has actually experienced it. Moreover, I did not know the full extent of the charges or issues being probed, and that only added to the fearful uncertainty of the whole experience.

I hired a well-respected Christian attorney in Chattanooga, Richard Bethea. I will forever be in his debt. I was able to bypass the personal guilt I felt in doing what we did, and addressing that was a part of preparing for the deposition. I agreed with Mr. Bethea that I would admit to nothing illegal and distance myself from it with careful and brief responses to questioning. It was clear from the beginning that they had a substantial case against the ministry, and I knew I was a willing participant in what we had done. I would validate their findings where that was necessary and be vague otherwise. My reputation, my wallet, and even potentially my freedom were at stake.

When the day of the deposition came, and I was ushered into the conference room, the sheer volume of the evidence they possessed stunned me. I had kept a few things, but they had copies of every confidential memo that I had and far, far beyond. It was clear that I was one of the last people they needed to speak with, and the depth of their evidence of the ministry's guilt in using ministry funds to help fund Pat's candidacy was overwhelming. That was evident in the questioning of the agents, but I can tell you as a witness that the stacks and stacks of incriminating documents was amazing. Their recall of events and the ability to pull a supporting document at a moment's notice was likewise impressive. I was a sitting duck, I knew it, and I was scared. Nevertheless, I think I did a good job of protecting myself and, to what extent I could, Pat and the ministry.

Excerpt from Terry Heaton Deposition

09/08/1988

IRS CID: How much input did Mr. Robertson have in the format of the show and the guests of the show?

Terry Heaton: He had very little regular input into what we did on the program. Pat's method of teaching and guiding the development of the program was to feed back after the show was over with. Prior to the show he basically let us do what we were taught and instructed to do. As far as him directly bringing guests in, uh...

IRS CID: Or suggesting guests?

TH: Or suggesting guests... I'm sure he did. I don't have any specific recollection of any particular person. I can't recall... this would be an example... I can't recall a name, but somebody was in town visiting with him or he would have breakfast with somebody and I remember one day he came in and said, "by the way, this guy's going to be on the show." As you can imagine, when you're trying to produce a live television program and everything... that's why I remember that. It's chaos at ten minutes to ten to all of a sudden to try and rebuild a 90-minute program. Yeah, he did bring people in but I don't know that they were specifically related to his political activities.

IRS CID: Did you have much of that? Did it change the run sheets for your show? Was this just an occasional occurrence maybe where he would introduce a guest to you at the last minute?

TH: Very occasional. The run sheets would change all the time because we just, uh... the other way Pat directed the production of the show was from the anchor chair. If you've got feature B planned to come up next, and he didn't feel like it should be feature B, then you'd go with something else. So we were flowing with the Holy Spirit, with what we felt the Holy Spirit was telling us to do with regards to the ministry aspects of the program. So, it was a "living format," that's what we always used to call it.

IRS CID: Okay. What about the format of the show? You said, when you came aboard, you interjected with a news background into the show whereas before it was primarily an entertainment...?

TH: No, it was a current events talk program more than anything. And, there was an occasional news piece in it but it wasn't the systematic news program that it evolved into in the 1980s.

IRS CID: This is the entire *700 Club* you're talking about?

TH: Yeah.

IRS CID: This was your idea then to interject the news features into?

TH: No, it wasn't my idea. I just, because of my background, knew how to do it. To explain that, CBN University has a film school that teaches people how to make films and they do it very well. But, there's a vast difference between making a film with a cast of thousands and 15 or 20 different people around and going out and doing a news story or magazine show story, a six-minute piece, and coming back and putting it together. That's where my experience came in, in helping teach people there how to do that.

IRS CID: So, your background was in news?

TH: News and magazines.

IRS CID: Is that one of the reasons you were hired? Were you given any kind of general direction when you were hired that they wanted it to be more of a news program?

TH: Yes.

IRS CID: By whom?

TH: Well, we had... by Michael Little, Rick Contana, who was one of the people involved in hiring me. By Pat. We would have planning retreats about once a year to look at the format of the show and review where we were growing and what we were trying to do with the program. The drift towards a news type of program was constant.

IRS CID: Let me ask you about the format again. The segment on _The 700 Club_ called "Pat's Perspectives"—when did that start on _The 700 Club_? Was that there when you took over as a senior editor or producer?

TH: No, you mean the part called, "Pat Robertson's Perspectives," where he sat at a blue and white set?

IRS CID: Well, I've seen several different ones, "Pat's Perspectives."

TH: I can't be sure of dates here but it seems to me we started that in... probably late 1985 and ended it in spring 1986.

IRS CID: Where did the idea come from? Did it come out of one of these meetings you attended?

TH: Yeah, the idea to do that specific segment was mine. You know, my responsibility was the ratings, the audience flow of the program, because revenue is directly tied to the universe that you're reaching. Uh, I reasoned, based upon my experience, that Pat's being off the program would have a detrimental effect on ratings. And, "Pat Robertson's Perspective,"... separating that from the rest of show allowed me to pre-tape segments, therefore allowing Pat to be on the show every day, even if he wasn't in Virginia Beach. Follow me?

IRS CID: What kind of topics did he present during "Pat's Perspectives"—what was the major...

TH: Same type of topics we used before "Pat's Perspective." News, current events, you know, told from a Judeo-Christian perspective. Anything from the economy, to Dungeons and Dragons. Alcoholism, drug addiction, marriage and family problems, foreign affairs...

IRS CID: We've looked at some of them and, of course, this is not a court of law, we're just gathering information and we gain perspectives and make assumptions from what we see. But, "Pat's Perspectives" strikes me as being a major vehicle whereby Mr. Robertson can make his potential platform known to people who are potential voters. Was this ever discussed, or anything like this ever discussed, during the course of "Pat's Perspectives" when you decided to put it on the air?

TH: No, because, again he was doing the same types of commentary outside of the window known as "Pat Robertson's Perspective." That whole thing was created for one purpose and one purpose only and, that was to assure that Pat would be on the program every day.

IRS CID: Because otherwise he was out traveling around somewhere...

TH: Right, and the show just was not the same without Pat.

IRS CID: Did he have any input...? You're right, throughout *The 700 Club* he goes up and presents these ideas on certain issues. Now, quite frankly, he gets into, close into the political arena. Whose ideas were those types of things? Did he have input into what he was going to say? Did someone always feed him a script and he just sat there and read it?

TH: Are you referring to his commentary, where he looks at the camera?

IRS CID: One that strikes me, let me see if I can remember this correctly. He was basically teaching Christians about the drift... Christians basically leaving the Democratic party and moving to the Republican party. This type of thing. There are other ones. That was one that just strikes my mind.

TH: That would be completely extemporaneous. No help at all from anybody. If he was to look at the camera and talk about that or to bring that up in a conversation with Ben or Danuta. Of course, if the subject you're referring to is from a "Pat Robertson's Perspective," there was no one there to bounce it off of, unless it was a guest. But, that was all his and it was unscripted.

....

IRS CID: Would you say that the guests that Pat had on the show were more conservative than liberal? There are several statements in the media that Pat never cared for the liberal press and that he was going to give a conservative slant to the news. I mean, you know, you look at some of the guests that appear on the show and the following of the conservative agenda. A lot of the different guests. Was any direction ever given to you as far as scheduling those types of guests—of a conservative bent?

TH: You've asked a couple of questions there.

IRS CID: I'll let you answer.

TH: If you took a look at the names of the people that appeared on the show in pre-produced news segments and as guests, I honestly think you'd come up with a pretty balanced list. As far as guests go... you asked a couple of questions... you asked, were there more conservative guests than liberals. Probably but I've not kept a record of that. You asked if I was instructed to do that. Not really but, when you're trying to do a program that offers a Biblical perspective on the news, I think, quite naturally you're going to end up in that direction.

IRS CID: Why is that?

TH: Well... (long pause) publicly those people espouse Biblical points of view more than people who would be classified as liberal. I'm uncomfortable with those two words anyway because I don't really know what they mean.

IRS CID: I guess... again... looking at the show and again... perceptions were growing... it appeared... you could make an argument that use was being made of *700 Club* to espouse mostly political issues or statements by bringing certain individuals. Again, we haven't watched all *The 700 Club*. So, what we're asking, in terms of the selection and the guests who were there, the topics presented, was there ever an understanding that you or *The 700 Club* should be espousing a certain position? Other than a purely Biblical C-3 [501c3] position?

TH: No, we were not ever instructed to espouse a specific political belief. Ours... we tried to be upfront about our bias being Biblical. And, you must understand, there were a lot of people that didn't want to be guests on *The 700 Club*. Maybe that was their perception, I don't know. But, no, we were not ever instructed to do that.

IRS CID: What about when you got into issues like funding the Contras, money going into Lebanon

and this kind of thing? Was there any kind of understanding that you had a position at CBN that you were supposed to take?

TH: Well, it's terribly oversimplified, but Contras and freedom and Nicaragua ... a case can be made for a Biblical perspective on that. At the heart of Communism is the hatred of God, and the evidence we had of things happening to evangelical ministers in Nicaragua. So that... if our position from a Biblical perspective lined up with one of two different political persuasions in the country, that's coincidence. Same thing for Lebanon, because of the value that evangelical Christians place on Israel and the Biblical significance of that country.

IRS CID: I'm not trying to put you onto... don't feel that you're... what you're saying is perfectly true. We're not in a C-3 engagement on some of this stuff. Is your response... is that the way most of the people at CBN felt or any of this direction coming specifically from Mr. Robertson?

TH: Well... you mean the Biblical perspective?

IRS CID: No, the support for certain things going on in the national or international scene.

IRS CID: Lebanon, Central America.

TH: I don't know how everybody else felt?

IRS CID: We can only ask for your opinion.

IRS CID: About your receiving instructions.

TH: By that, do you mean, I was told "do this story because..." You know, I'm just having trouble framing words here. I think, I know I felt a certain compassion for the Contras from a Biblical perspective. I felt the same way about the people of Israel. And I didn't think it any big deal that we were doing stories to that effect. I was never instructed "you will do this because this is something, in particular areas, that I want to do." That's what your question really is.

....

IRS CID: Do you know about the 501C3 Prohibition against substantial lobbying?

TH: Yes, I do.

IRS CID: The reason I'm asking about this particular one in March of '86 with General Singlaub on the show is in, there was about a twenty-minute portion of the show devoted entirely to the Contra Aid Bill and the support of it, in which the Capitol switchboard number was given for the general

audience to call. Now, this is lobbying. Who came up with this guest?

TH: It's not illegal to do some of that correct? So, we did put the Capitol switchboard number up from time to time. Very careful to say, whatever your opinion is, it is your Constitutional duty and your right as a citizen to let your Congressman or your Representative know how you feel about it. Very careful to do that.

IRS CID: Can I take it a step further? Some other people have said this but they've also said you know the audience you're playing for... we know that conservative Christians generally will probably take a certain position. Was that a well known fact also with *700 Club* staff that chances were, this is what you were doing. And, again, lobbying... a certain amount of this is legal but I'm trying to get an understanding of the way you operate.

TH: I can't... again, I can't answer for everybody else, but I knew.

IRS CID: When you did these things, were these things cleared with Pat before you would flash this thing on the screen... the number. Was he aware of it in advance that you were going to be doing this?

TH: Generally speaking, the impetus to put the Capitol switchboard phone number up or the White House phone number came from Pat Robertson during the show.

IRS CID: So he would make the decision while you were taping?

TH: While we were live with millions of people.

IRS CID: You're live... your morning show is live.

TH: Remember I told you it was a living format. We had those things... those phone numbers were kept in our still store. Just like a lot of other things were kept in our still store. When he called for it... sometimes he would even give us the blessing of telling us in the dressing room that he wanted to do it. He didn't surprise us out on the floor.

IRS CID: So, generally speaking, he was the one who gave the direction to flash that number so people would call?

TH: Yes sir.

IRS CID: Do you know if he ever supported candidates on the air or guests brought on *The 700 Club* that were up for office? Or if... candidates that were not conservative...if *The 700 Club* would give

alternate candidate. In other words, try to discredit that candidate... specifically speaking about Mrs. Bird out in California, the judge.

TH: This is the one... Rose Bird.

IRS CID: She's justice of California Supreme Court.

TH: We're not these vicious people who set about to you know destroy people for election. We didn't do that kind of thing. Did we have guests on who were running for office? I just don't see how you can do news without some-times doing that but I really don't know.

IRS CID: We know but don't miss the point. I guess the point... you did some segments which were basically anti-Bird in the show. Again, in that specific instance, who... where did that come from? That idea to do that show? Did that come from the [?] or someone else?

TH: More than likely that would come from staff. To do a story that would...

Bethea: Terry, what they're asking is if you know. If you know where this came from. Tell them if you don't know.

TH: I really don't.

This kind of questioning went on for three hours, and I was exhausted when all was said and done. I learned a valuable lesson about the government's ability to obtain incriminating evidence against anybody. The idea—especially in this day and age—of operating entirely "in secret" is really quite preposterous.

As noted, I was back in local television news at the time of this deposition, and I was curious about it as a reporter. Who wouldn't be? Pat Robertson had attended school in Chattanooga, so there was a local element to anything newsworthy involving the man.

IRS CID agent Ford Allen had given me his business card at the deposition, so I called him early in 1989 to inquire about the investigation. He told me that it had been dropped. I was completely caught off guard by his answer. He declined to tell me more, only that the order to do so had come "from the highest of higher-ups." My assumption for this has always been that Bush called off the dogs for Pat's endorsement to the "religious right" of the Republican Party. I can't prove that, and I've not had the wherewithal to investigate it.

Whatever happened, it wasn't permanent. In 1998, CBN paid a "significant" fine to the IRS for illegal activities in 1985 and 1986 that cost the ministry its tax-exempt status for 1986 and 1987.[19] In 1992, the Federal Election Commission hit Americans for Robertson with a repayment order for $388,500 in the wake of its audit investigation.[20]

Seven

CBN News, Fox News, and the Matter of Transparency

Never pick a fight with people who buy ink by the barrel.
—Mark Twain

Television news—and other forms of journalism of the future—will steadily drift away from the "professional" standard of objectivity and back to one that regularly incorporates argument into its soul. If you study postmodernism, this conclusion is inevitable, and it will produce—I predict—a change in the culture as significant and lasting as the American Revolution. Moreover, this change will occur outside the institution of journalism and in spite of its ongoing self-examination.

To even begin understanding the dynamics of this change, one must first leave the safe pedestal of professionalism. This is why the institution will never "get it" and why the ultimate arrival of the new age will seem sudden, when it really has been bubbling and simmering for decades. So set aside everything you've been taught and believe, and let's take a little trip back in time. If journalism is the first rough draft of history, then who were the first journalists?

Since the dawn of humanity, cultures have carried their myths and histories with them. These accounts reflected not only factual occurrences but also the cultural contexts within which they took place. As such, none would pass the muster of today's standards, because journalism goes beyond storytelling and includes, I believe, an element of investigation—an attempt to satisfy curiosity brought about by questions. This is the integral assumption upon which journalism is built and the missing element in much of today's junk.

Let's open the New Testament for a moment. The gospel accounts of the story of Jesus carry similar story lines, but Luke—a physician who also wrote the book of Acts—adds elements that the others don't. Take a look at the way he begins his account:

> Most honorable Theophilus: Many people have written accounts about the events that took place among us. They used as their source material the reports circulating among us from the early disciples and other eyewitnesses of what God has done in fulfillment of his promises. Having carefully investigated all of these accounts from the beginning, I have decided to write a careful summary for you, to reassure you of the truth of all you were taught. (Luke 1: 1-4 NLT)

This is remarkably similar to the origins of "newsletters," those accounts of commerce in distant lands sent back to the merchants who paid for the service. A "reporter" studied and investigated and then wrote an account of what he found. This was the beginning of journalism, and it forms the core task of the trade.

Napoleon conquered Europe, yet he wrote, "Four hostile newspapers are more to be feared than a thousand bayonets." Revolutionary War era newspapers, many of which were shut down by the British for espousing their views, influenced the writing of the First Amendment, so that such opposition would never again be silenced in the new world. Facts don't need constitutional protection, but ideas certainly do. It is why the Israelis work so hard to control their narrative, even going to great lengths to censor YouTube, Facebook, and other forms of horizontal communications over what they view as "incitement."

The assassination of President Abraham Lincoln provides a useful look into the mind of mid-nineteenth century journalism. A *New York Herald* dispatch from Washington regarding the execution of the four who conspired with John Wilkes Booth contained the following:

> The execution of his murderers today has proven us to be a law-abiding people; otherwise the miscreants who plotted and executed their great crime would have long since been torn to pieces by the people, who were as much convinced of their guilt before as after their trial. Everything has been done decently and in order, and the majesty of the law and of the nation has been vindicated, and the guiltiest of the wretches have gone to answer for their crimes at the great tribunal where no subterfuge will avail to hide their criminality.

Not much objectivity there. One of the four hanged was female. The reporter justified her death by painting a portrait of a woman devoid of femininity.

> (Her) gray eyes were cold and lifeless and added to the masculinity of her appearance. They were seldom lit up by excitement or pleasure, though occasionally they gleamed with a furious or stealthy glare which indexed the bad passions of her soul...She appears to have been masculine not only in person and manners, but in mind.[21]

The point is that the roots of journalism do not include the pristine notion that one should (or even could) stand far off and report facts without opinion or "argument"—to use historian Christopher Lasch's term. "The job of the press is to encourage debate," he wrote in *The Lost Art of Political Argument* for *Harper's* in 1990, "not to supply the public with information." He espoused the idea that argument precedes understanding and is central to democratic opinion formation. And democratic opinion was the issue that split liberal thinkers in the years following World War I, when the modern public relations era was born. One group, led by Pragmatic philosopher John Dewey, believed that the public could and should participate in democracy. Walter Lippmann, the man who would later be called the "Dean of American Journalism," headed the other group and maintained that the public was too ignorant to do any more than cast ballots once in a while.

The idea that the public might intrude into the affairs of "responsible men" was repugnant to the cynical Lippmann, who voiced his social engineering vision in two important books, *Public Opinion* (1922) and *The Phantom Public* (1925):

> A false ideal of democracy can only lead to disillusionment and to meddlesome tyranny. If democracy cannot direct affairs, then a philosophy which expects it to direct them will encourage the people to attempt the impossible; they will fail...The public must be put in its place, so that it may exercise its own powers, but no less and perhaps even more, so that each of us may live free of the trampling and the roar of a bewildered herd.[22]

He deplored what he saw as the uneducated manipulating the masses through the use of symbols and stereotypes and called for an educated elite to run things on behalf of everybody. Thus was born the "professional" journalist, one who was free of symbol and stereotype and would assist the other elite institutions in leading the country, something Lippmann had already done as an advisor to President Woodrow Wilson.

Dewey, on the other hand, was a firm believer that the open exchange of ideas permitted the people to govern themselves:

> The act of voting is in a democratic regime a culmination of a continued process of open and public communication in which prejudices have the opportunity to erase each other; that continued interchange of facts and ideas exposes what is unsound and discloses what may make for human well-being...Any fair-minded survey of suppressive acts in

this country will demonstrate that their ultimate source is always a privileged minority (with the majority standing passively by and permitting it to occur).[23]

The postmodern mind is eerily similar to Dewey's and immediately repelled by Lippmann's. Postmoderns look around and see ruin where the elites promised prosperity. The American Dream lives on only for the few, and the resulting anti-institutional energy is fierce and unrelenting. Technology has leveled the knowledge playing field and thrust the masses into unfamiliar territory, where the application of knowledge used to be reserved only for the few. The rational command and control of modernism is under assault by people who find greater comfort in anarchy than what they view as the false promise of the shepherds.

The bitter animosity expressed today between the political right and left overwhelmed social media during the 2016 presidential campaign. This was a part of what Dewey was addressing, for the extremes tend to cancel each other out. Facts don't need hyperbole. That's reserved for opinions, and we all need to come to grips with the notion that the airing of these viewpoints is a necessary part of finding agreement. What we have today, however, is not what we'll have tomorrow, for we've only just begun. This assumes, of course, that the net can remain free.

We need to teach journalistic responsibility and ethics in elementary school, for we are all now journalists—observers—in the network.

CBN News played a pioneering role in the development and growth of new point-of-view journalism when I was producer of *The 700 Club*. In 1982, commentator Ron Powers criticized a CBN News story in a segment on *CBS Sunday Morning*. I was watching as Powers made the incredible statement that the piece "was so slanted that it was vertical." Of course it was, and we never advertised it as being anything else. Our slogan was "TV Journalism with a Different Spirit," and we made no bones about what "different spirit" we were referencing.

In talking about CBN News, I use the word "we" cautiously, for I officially had only an advisory role with this talented group of people. This was one of those management matters about which much has already been written, for in an attempt to create an ethical wall of separation between news and the ministry, CBN News was created as a separate division with an independent chain of command. Like many other things, that separation was strictly for show, because it fell apart completely in practice. Perhaps it gave management a useful talking point in dealing with outsiders, but what was said and what was done were quite often very different.

Pat Robertson was the absolute authority of CBN, and that expectation could overrule anything that the organizational chart produced. So no matter what was said in the ranks, Pat Robertson was the executive editor of CBN News. As I have tried to stress elsewhere, the proximity to Pat within my daily responsibilities put me in a difficult position with others. The simple truth is he would say things to me that he wouldn't say to others, and he expected me not to say "Pat said" as a qualifier for instructions I passed to those contributing to the television program.

This in and of itself put me at odds with those in CBN's news department. If, for example, I offered any comment perceived as negative about any particular report, or if I were to offer a suggestion, the defensive response would be to ask whether this was my own thinking or if it had come from Pat. I felt always the middleman, although I was one of the very few people at the ministry who had actually worked as a manager in television news and magazine shows prior to affiliation with CBN. I cut my news teeth in the very difficult news market of Milwaukee, but managers of the news department rejected the experience and the views and practices I had learned. Perhaps it was my personality or the way in which I attempted to share that knowledge, but regardless, I never once felt like anything other than an adversary to them.

And that was really a shame, for their purpose was my purpose, and the newsy edge that their material created for opening the show was always my favorite part. I have referred to CBN News and my experiences many times in my work over the past fifteen years. Before Fox News was, there was CBN News, which gives me unique insight into the criticism leveled at Fox News by the journalism community at large. I think the only thing that's "wrong" with Fox News is that they are not transparent about their efforts to provide a cultural balance for journalism.

Hence, it comes off as shilling for the Republican Party, because in many ways it is. The "balance" that Fox attempts to provide is in its inclusion of viewpoints considered outside that which the press labels the "sphere of consensus." There is, however, a distance between what they're attempting to do and what they're actually presenting. Fox may present a balancing factor in press coverage of the news overall, but their perspective is entirely conservative, Republican, and Christian. No attempt is made to include the liberal point-of-view—except as pejorative—and this is why they are not transparent with their bias.

Daniel C. Hallin's book about Vietnam, *The Uncensored War*, offers deep insight into the decision-making processes of the press. By offering expanding circles defining three "spheres" of press influence: the sphere of consensus, the sphere of legitimate controversy, and the sphere of deviance. Here is the way Hallin envisioned it[24]:

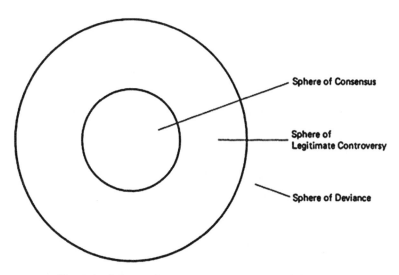

Figure 1 Spheres of consensus, controversy, and deviance.

According to Hallin, these three regions define the Washington journalist's world. The centermost sphere of consensus is where journalists feel no need to provide forms of argument, for the subjects here are not regarded as controversial. Hallin wrote, "Within this region journalists do not feel compelled either to present opposing views or to remain disinterested observers. On the contrary," he added, "the journalist's role is to serve as an advocate or celebrant of consensus values."

Just outside consensus exists the sphere of legitimate controversy, where objectivity and balance rule, especially as it regards the process for electing our representatives and the two-party system. Opposing views are required, because the subjects themselves are considered controversial.

The outer realm Hallin calls the sphere of deviance, where subjects and actors exist that society's political mainstream reject as "unworthy of being heard," according to Hallin. Neutrality doesn't exist in this realm, and the press is free to decide who resides here, because such players are considered beyond "acceptable political conflict."

This is especially useful analysis today in examining what happened with the election of Donald Trump, for a great many people sense that their views are considered deviant by a liberally-biased press. Where the status quo is considered consensus, those who disagree are seen as deviant, and this doesn't sit well with those who feel powerless as a result.

Both Fox News and CBN News thumb their nose at this and shout that being shuttled to the sphere of deviance is bias, and they are absolutely correct. This is the real problem that those who refuse to march in lockstep with the culture are fighting constantly in trying to inform others of perspectives embraced by significant groups of people.

This further makes the Fox News position of "fair and balanced" ridiculous, for Fox presents its own spheres of consensus, legitimate controversy, and deviance. The entire product is a form of point-of-view journalism. If they instead offered a slogan and mission statement outlining the beliefs and social conclusions, it would pose an entirely different and more acceptable challenge to observers who follow the news.

In all the world, nobody understands this better than Harvard's great "knowledge thinker" David Weinberger, who in July of 2009 penned his original thinking in a widely-referenced blog post called "Transparency is the new objectivity." It is reprinted here with permission:

> A friend asked me to post an explanation of what I meant when I said at PDF09 that "transparency is the new objectivity." First, I apologize for the cliché of "x is the new y." Second, what I meant is that transparency is now fulfilling some of objectivity's old role in the ecology of knowledge.
>
> Outside of the realm of science, objectivity is discredited these days as anything but an aspiration, and even that aspiration is looking pretty sketchy. The problem with objectivity is that it tries to show what the world looks like from no particular point of view, which is like wondering what something looks like in the dark. Nevertheless, objectivity—even as an unattainable goal—served an important role in how we came to trust information, and in the economics of newspapers in the modern age.

You can see this in newspapers' early pushback against blogging. We were told that bloggers have agendas, whereas journalists give us objective information. Of course, if you don't think objectivity is possible, then you think that the claim of objectivity is actually hiding the biases that inevitably are there. That's what I meant when, during a bloggers press conference at the 2004 Democratic National Convention, I asked Pulitzer-prize winning journalist Walter Mears whom he was supporting for president. He replied (paraphrasing!), "If I tell you, how can you trust what I write?" to which I replied that if he doesn't tell us, how can we trust what he blogs?

So, that's one sense in which transparency is the new objectivity. What we used to believe because we thought the author was objective we now believe because we can see through the author's writings to the sources and values that brought her to that position. Transparency gives the reader information by which she can undo some of the unintended effects of the ever-present biases. Transparency brings us to reliability the way objectivity used to. This change is epochal.

Objectivity used to be presented as a stopping point for belief: If the source is objective and well-informed, you have sufficient reason to believe. The objectivity of the reporter is a stopping point for reader's inquiry. That was part of high-end newspapers' claimed value: You can't believe what you read in a slanted tabloid, but our news is objective, so your inquiry can come to rest here.

Credentialing systems had the same basic rhythm: You can stop your quest once you come to a credentialed authority who says, "I got this. You can believe it." End of story.

We thought that that was how knowledge works, but it turns out that it's really just how paper works. Transparency prospers in a linked medium, for you can literally see the connections between the final draft's claims and the ideas that informed it. Paper, on the other hand, sucks at links. You can look up the footnote, but that's an expensive, time-consuming activity more likely to result in failure than success. So, during the Age of Paper, we got used to the idea that authority comes in the form of a stop sign: You've reached a source whose reliability requires no further inquiry.

In the Age of Links, we still use credentials and rely on authorities. Those are indispensable ways of scaling knowledge, that is, letting us know more than any one of us could authenticate on our own. But, increasingly, credentials and authority work best for vouchsafing commoditized knowledge, the stuff that's settled and not worth arguing about. At the edges of knowledge—in the analysis and contextualization that journalists nowadays tell us is their real value—we want, need, can have, and expect transparency. Transparency puts within the report itself a way for us to see what assumptions and values may have shaped it, and lets us see the arguments that the report resolved one way and not another. Transparency—the embedded ability to see through the published draft—often gives us more reason to believe a report than the claim of objectivity did.

In fact, transparency subsumes objectivity. Anyone who claims objectivity should be willing to back that assertion up by letting us look at sources, disagreements, and the personal assumptions and values supposedly bracketed out of the report.

Objectivity without transparency increasingly will look like arrogance. And then foolishness. Why should we trust what one person—with the best of intentions—insists is true when we instead could have a web of evidence, ideas, and argument?

In short: Objectivity is a trust mechanism you rely on when your medium can't do links. Now our medium can.[25]

Walter Lippmann's vision of professional journalism was cynical and self-serving. In order to sell space in the paper to advertisers (and become very much the wealthy elitists that Lippmann so admired), the content had to be presented in as sterile a manner as possible. Hence, the concept of objectivity was born and eventually the hallmark of journalism across the industry.

In the mid twentieth century, two events occurred during the presidency of Richard Nixon that altered the very notion of what it meant to be a journalist. On November 13, 1969, Vice President Spiro Agnew addressed Republicans in Des Moines, Iowa, taking on the press, especially television news. Known as Nixon's "hatchet man," Agnew had a history of making highly controversial public remarks, and his "law and order" approach helped soothe an electorate frightened by disruptive events at the Democratic National Convention in Chicago in 1968. In this speech, he assigned power and influence to television news in such a way that it fueled the imaginations of every would-be news reporter throughout the land.

> Tonight I want to discuss the importance of the television medium to the American people. No nation depends more on the intelligent judgment of its citizens. And no medium has a more profound influence over public opinion. Nowhere in our system are there fewer checks on such vast power. So nowhere should there be more conscientious responsibility exercised than by the news media. The question is, Are we demanding enough of our television news presentations? And are the men of this medium demanding enough of themselves?

Agnew went on to discuss an important speech by Nixon on the Vietnam War that he felt was rejected by the television commentators who presented the speech on their networks.

> Every American has a right to disagree with the President of the United States and to express publicly that disagreement.
>
> But the president of the United States has a right to communicate directly with the people who elected him, and the people of this country have the right to make up their own minds and form their own opinions about a

presidential address without having the president's words
and thoughts characterized through the prejudices of hostile critics before they can even be digested.

He spoke of the reach of the networks and provided statistics that
led to his conclusion that unchecked power in the hands of so few
was dangerous for the country.

For millions of Americans the network reporter who covers
a continuing issue, like ABM or civil rights, becomes, in
effect, the presiding judge in a national trial by jury.
    …A raised eyebrow, an inflection of the voice, a
caustic remark dropped in the middle of a broadcast can
raise doubts in a million minds about the veracity of a
public official or the wisdom of a Government policy.
    …it represents a concentration of power over American
public opinion unknown in history.[26]

This speech did nothing to alter the truth of Agnew's claims;
it actually made things worse, for now the public, including its
journalists, had a new vision about the calling of the press—to be
power brokers alongside those elites they were assigned to cover.
    This led directly to the second event that forever altered
what it meant to be a journalist in America—the Watergate
scandal—and the efforts of two *Washington Post* reporters, Bob
Woodward and Carl Bernstein. It turns out that the "hero" of
the whole mess was a disgruntled, high-ranking FBI executive that fed information to Woodward and Bernstein, but that

didn't stop the glorification of the reporting process that took down a sitting US president.

The public was curious about Watergate, but a press that was in love with the story overwhelmed that curiosity. It remains the biggest "gotcha" story in the history of journalism, and it single-handedly turned reporting into a career of celebrity and glory. As Wikipedia tells it in an article about Woodward and Bernstein, "Their book about the scandal, *All the President's Men*, became a Number One bestseller and was later turned into a movie. The 1976 film, starring Robert Redford as Woodward and Dustin Hoffman as Bernstein, transformed the reporters into celebrities and inspired a wave of interest in investigative journalism."

I watched as this played out over the next few decades from my position as an interested participant and observer. It was rampant in the hearts and minds of people who interviewed for news jobs at the many television stations where I worked as a news executive. It was the very pinnacle of the dream of modernity, to walk among the haves on the job and often socially. Television, especially, became the easiest path to celebrity in the guise of the public interest. Walter Lippmann's "professionalism" was revealed for what it actually was, a way to manipulate and be manipulated through one's ego. Eventually, those same public figures learned how to play the game and take advantage of this self-interest to manipulate the process of news. I have, for example, an animal rights magazine from the 1990s that contains an article outlining—point by accurate point—how to successfully approach and manipulate a local TV station for news coverage.

Of all the things that the press obscures in the gathering and reporting of news, this career self-interest bothers me most. Many, if not most, of the reporting staff at any local news operation don't really want to be there. Each TV station is viewed as a stepping-stone to a bigger market, and so many enter through the front door with one foot already out the back. Their work in the smaller market includes the strong motivation to do highly flamboyant pieces for their résumé tape that will quickly grab the attention of a "more important" news director elsewhere. It is why the farm system for local TV news is corrupt. The business is almost entirely self-centered and self-driven.

This is yet another reason why transparency is the new objectivity, because the public is increasingly onto this fact. As David Weinberger wrote, "Objectivity without transparency increasingly will look like arrogance. And then foolishness."

In the future, journalism will select vertical topics of interest, which will make transparency much easier to show. We will also see the subjects of verticals increasingly transparent, because they'll be rejected as advertising otherwise. This all seems remarkably chaotic to those accustomed to modernity's equilibrium, but we'll learn and adapt, because we won't have any choice. Frankly, I'd prefer a little chaos to the nonsense that continues to pass itself off as objective news.

There's much being written today about the Internet as an echo chamber in which people simply choose to entertain only those outside thoughts that conform to their existing thinking. This fear assumes that this can never and will never change, but the very structure of the Web itself cannot tolerate black and white for long. Search and the ever present linking to supporting documentation will eventually crack the very foundation of circling the wagons.

CBN News and Fox News feed this isolation of thinking in ways that are both useful and damaging to the culture. There is no doubt that there are many conservatives who do not embrace the far limits of the right, and they deserve a voice in the public square. Likewise, there are those liberals who do not embrace the far limits of the left, and they, too, deserve a voice. Extremes tend to cancel themselves out, as we're witnessing today with a slate full of Republican Party candidates for president that are being pulled to the right despite cries for moderation from the party itself and many of the people who support it. This is because the most vocal wing of the Republican Party represents the Evangelical Christians who are in it for reasons beyond reason. Their zealotry leads the way in expressing extreme conservative "values" in all matters pertaining to social mores, and their minds are closed to discussion. They subscribe to those sites that continually pump out memes that fit their point of view, so that these people can pass them along without question via social media and the Internet as a whole.

Here are just a few popular examples from 2015, some quoted verbatim, from various sites. Each is completely false:

The Bachmann story

"Marcus Bachmann, husband of former Minnesota Congresswoman Michele Bachmann, unwittingly became the first public face of

Indiana's newly-enacted Religious Freedom Restoration Act, after being refused service at a dress boutique because the store owner assumed he was gay."[27]

The German pilot story

"All evidence indicates that the copilot of Airbus machine in his six-months break during his training as a pilot in Germanwings, converted to Islam and subsequently either by the order of 'radical,' ie. devout Muslims, or received the order from the book of terror, the Quran, on his own accord decided to carry out this mass murder. As a radical mosque in Bremen in which the convert was often staying is at the center of the investigation, it can be assumed that he—as Mohammed Atta, in the attack against New York—received his instructions directly from the immediate vicinity of the mosque."[28]

Ask Dr. Brown[29]

Dr. Michael Brown is a Christian evangelist with a radio program and a prolific online ministry that pumps out meme after meme for Facebook users to pass along. In one designed to demonstrate that Israel is the only country in the Middle East that gives women full political rights, he used a 2004 photograph from a military parade in Iraq where women marched as a group dressed all in black and wearing veils over their heads. This was deliberately designed to represent *all* Muslim women in the Middle East. A converted Jew, Dr. Brown is a relentless supporter of Israel, and many of his memes reflect that belief. This terribly misleading picture was "shared" by over 8,000 of his followers.

White baby hurt in racial attack

Nearly every conservative website ran the story of a black teen who attacked a white classmate who was holding her toddler at the time. The story garnered widespread attention via social media, because a photo of a baby with a bad cut over his right eye accompanied the text. The image was shocking juxtaposed with a theme of racial violence. It turned out to be bogus—the actual child accompanying the victim was older. The damage, however, had been done.[30]

Arabs react to President Obama

The YouTube site "iPhone Conservative" posted a video[31] made by Memritv.org with a highly controversial translation of comments made by Arab television personalities allegedly reacting to a speech by President Obama. According to its website, translation is Memritv's core competency:

> The Middle East Media Research Institute (MEMRI) was founded in 1998 in Washington, DC to bridge the language gap between the Middle East and the West by monitoring, translating, and studying Arab, Iranian and Turkish media, schoolbooks, and religious sermons.

Unfortunately, the translation is entirely false, and yet it received over three million views in just eight months. The allegations presented were deemed to be false by the fact-checking website Snopes.[32]

Snopes is a fascinating online company, and I've often wondered why it is the lone debunker of an increasingly pesky problem for the online journalism community. No longer is it sufficient for journalists to be only responsible for what they personally research and write. Without including deviations, we unwittingly open the door for the fringes, and this has been taking place for many years. Smart marketers have discovered the reality that people will pass along their nonsense via social media, because fraudulent reporting fits so well in belief systems searching for validation.

There are three new news beats that every media company should be exploring:

- Fakes & Memes
- Changing culture (disruptions)
- Technology and the people who use it

The *Washington Post* took on fakes and memes in a nineteen-month experiment that ended in December of 2015. "What was fake on the internet this week" was encouraging not only in the scope of its mission but also in the wonderful way it was written by Caitlin Dewey, and the decision to end the column was extremely disappointing. Believing the pace and tenor of fake news had changed, here's how Dewey expressed the decision in her final column:

> ...where a willingness to believe hoaxes once seemed to come from a place of honest ignorance or misunderstanding, that's frequently no longer the case...
>
> ...There's a simple, economic explanation for this shift: If you're a hoaxer, it's more profitable. Since early

2014, a series of Internet entrepreneurs have realized that not much drives traffic as effectively as stories that vindicate and/or inflame the biases of their readers. Where many once wrote celebrity death hoaxes or "satires," they now run entire, successful websites that do nothing but troll convenient minorities or exploit gross stereotypes. Paul Horner, the proprietor of Nbc.com.co and a string of other very profitable fake-news sites, once told me he specifically tries to invent stories that will provoke strong reactions in middle-aged conservatives. They share a lot on Facebook, he explained; they're the ideal audience...

...Needless to say, there are also more complicated, non-economic reasons for the change on the Internet hoax beat. For evidence, just look at some of the viral stories we've debunked in recent weeks: American Muslims rallying for ISIS, for instance, or Syrians invading New Orleans. Those items didn't even come from outright fake-news sites: They originated with partisan bloggers who know how easy it is to profit off fear-mongering.

Frankly, this column wasn't designed to address the current environment.[33]

Dewey went on the say that it feels "a little pointless" and noted that institutional distrust is so high and cognitive bias so strong that hoax news stories are consumed by those only interested in information that confirms their views, "even when it's demonstrably false."

She promises that the *Washington Post* isn't finished with the hoax beat, but will be producing something different in the future.

I, for one, am glad to see that, because this is an enormous problem for journalism and for the culture itself.

As noted earlier in this book, it isn't the leaders of the extremes that we should fear; it's the followers, and our obligation is to them. We're going to need a way to present fake news and hoaxes that does not threaten the deeply held convictions and fears of those followers.

Meanwhile, those lockstep supporters of the Christian right hang on for dear life to the twisted and self-serving "facts" presented by Fox News and CBN News in the name of being a good Christian. They deny their ignorance and cite Biblical references like I Corinthians 1:27 (NIV): "God has chosen the foolish things of the world that He might shame the wise." This gives a bizarre form of license to the followers of those who seek political gain. It is volatile and dangerous, and while conservatives scream about the horrors of political correctness today, there's a much greater horror in place in the US today, and that's the fear of stepping on the toes of the very people who complain about "liberal" political correctness. After all, they're extremely well organized, and their leaders know precisely how to rile the troops to flood website comments and gain signatures on petitions to the FCC, the Judiciary, Congress, and the White House. This is a fruit of the gospel of self.

Modern Christianity is not above reproach, and unless we talk about the basics with each other, we're going to see the cultural gaps between the absolutes of justice and mercy get even wider. This begins with real transparency from any person or thing calling itself a "news" organization. And that leads to perhaps the biggest revelation in examining the very basis of any group calling itself a "news" organization. It begins with separating news from politics, and in this sense, we can see that so-called "right wing media" isn't really in the news business at all. Thus, the narrative that drives them is completely false.

Recall Spiro Agnew's proclamation that the president ought to be able to speak directly to the American people without going through what he viewed as a liberal filter, one that would distort Nixon's views through its blurred lens. Nixon's was the first conservative administration in the golden age of television, and it struggled with its inability to control the message during an incredibly volatile time in history. Many others took up the claim in the wake of Watergate. After all, only a political opponent would strive to take down a sitting president, surely not a press that advertised itself as objective.

These complaints fell on deaf ears, because the complainers lacked a media stage from which to make their case. As a result, they had to rely on that same blurred lens, so efforts to "speak against liberals" were dead before they started. We had such a stage at CBN, one of the original ten transponders on the first RCA communications satellite, Satcom One. Moreover, ours was a video show, and we had the production chops to create whatever we wanted along the artificial plane known as political perspective. It didn't matter that the press didn't really belong on this plane, only that it was convenient for our purposes, which we claimed to be preparing the world for the return of Jesus Christ.

So we publicly moved "the press" in its entirety to the left on this political plane in order to insert a convenient fence on its right edge. We placed ourselves (and the ilk of Rush Limbaugh, etc.) to the right of that fence, which gave the appearance of the bigger overall culture being represented under the banner of "news." After all, most people were either liberal or conservative politically, and politics—or *influencing* politics—was our real goal. I can't possibly overstate this reality. You do not change the world by changing the press; you simply must make the case that the press isn't neutral, and the rest is easy. The press, of course, helped us with this, because it was easy to pick news coverage hooks that represented a more progressive view of culture for us to hone in on. We were free to assign bias even in cases where the press was simply doing its job.

Dog bites man, it's not news. Man bites dog, it's news. This simple old metaphor points to the false narrative we created, because the very definition of news is tied to that which is different, that which is, well, "new." And new always means progressive, for basic conservative logic is tied to the status quo and the maintenance of tradition and its accompanying hierarchies. Many if not most journalists are educated, passionate about their trade, and ethical when it comes to the rules of professional observation. Only in the sense that some of this can be applied to "liberalism" is the press liberal. It is a fake moniker given to them without their consent by people who need it to be that way in order to fit their own self-serving narrative. There is no conspiracy. Journalists don't regularly gather to discuss how they're going to manipulate unknowing masses with lies and deceit. That is much more likely to be found with those who claim participation in "right wing media."

On abortion, for example, Evangelical Christians almost always leave out the original pioneers in the pro-life movement, the Catholics. This is an important element in understanding right wing media, for the Catholic Church is hardly conservative. In addition to calling out the pro-choicers for what was actually taking place in the wake of Roe v. Wade, Catholics also pleaded the cause of those "unwanted" babies after they were born, and also opposed the death penalty. That, my friends, is the very definition of pro-life. Catholics also tended to vote for the left, so their voice in the debate about abortion carried far more weight than that of any other group. But that voice didn't fit the narrative of the right, and the squeaky wheel gets the grease. In seizing upon abortion as an Evangelical Christian cause, the political right gained an emotional grassroots appeal to which it was not entitled. You can't claim to be "pro-life" and not plead the cause of the poor and the oppressed or those sitting on death row, unless, of course, your gospel is the gospel of self. The same thing applies to many of the right's causes, because political power is the real goal.

The mere suggestion that manipulation can result in rolling back laws that are tagged as culturally offensive to some is folly and a chasing of the wind. This includes the idea that if only conservatives could appoint enough Supreme Court justices, they will eventually overturn Roe v. Wade. The odds of this ever happening are remarkably small for many reasons, and wishers would do well to consider that the original opinion in Roe v. Wade was written by conservative justice Harry Blackmun, a Nixon appointee to the court. Nevertheless, right wing media needs to continually dangle this carrot in order to maintain the hyperbole of its claims as members of the press, albeit with a different worldview.

Right wing media is not, nor will it ever be, a part of the press, for its core purpose is the manipulation of culture through distortion, the very thing it assigns to the so-called "liberal" media. Moreover, many contemporary right wing media outlets are nothing more than political operatives with the sole purpose of repeating over and over again their purely political arguments. To this end, nothing is out-of-bounds, for baseless and provable lies are fair game in a sea of ethical emptiness. Again, the irony is that these groups practice out loud the very things they accuse their political opponents of doing in disguise, as if that somehow justifies deliberately "balancing" the public square by any means necessary. Even when bona fide "fact checker" organizations prove beyond a reasonable doubt the falsity of certain claims, these political hacks continue to repeat the allegations, presumably because they feel under no obligation to retract or otherwise accept responsibility for such lies. Moreover, they know that as long as they can keep the drum beating, there are people "out there" who've been trained to listen regardless of the evidence.

The press is a political animal only insofar as it covers politics, and even I have to admit there can be mischief in this particular hen house. New York University journalism professor and author Jay Rosen has been studying this for thirty years and refers to the Washington press corps in particular as the "national press or political press." He argues strongly for transparency and accountability and against opacity and demagoguery. He is also acutely aware of the difference between "journalism" and this "political press."

If your job is to make the case, win the negotiations, decide what the community should do, or maintain morale, that is one kind of work. If your job is to tell people what's going on, and equip them to participate without illusions, that is a very different kind of work.

The press is the latter and politics is the former. Right wing media, however, claims to be the latter while functioning as the former, and this is why its narrative is a fraud. Again, there is no such thing as "right wing media." It is entirely political, and we shouldn't stand for it. Drudge is not a journalist. Hannity is not a journalist. Limbaugh is not a journalist. A thousand websites with "news" in their titles are not practicing journalism whatsoever. They are like the local advertiser who presents his commercial message during the six o'clock news disguised as a news bulletin. There are ethical rules against this, but in desperate times, there are also exceptions.

Finally, nearly every attempt to create a "left wing media"— to put a fence to the left of the press—has failed, the most visible being Al Franken's program on the Air America Network. Billed as an alternative to conservative talk radio, Franken's show never garnered the ratings of his counterparts on the right and certainly didn't inspire a generation of progressive radio talk shows. While there are a handful of successful progressive programs today, there doesn't appear to be a wellspring of an audience for this fare, perhaps because it's so obviously there only to counter the right.

Right or left, these "media" are political activists and not members of any journalistic effort whatsoever. We have got our work cut out for us, if we are to educate the public about how we've been duped and manipulated by smart political operatives, those who only have their own best interests in mind. We pioneered this in Virginia Beach, and while our motives may have seemed to be just at the time, the truth is we were just another group of social engineers with the political motivations of power and influence.

The press is a part of the media, but media is not the press, for we are all media players today.

Eight

Pat Robertson's Influence Today

"I'm so proud of everything you're doing."
—Pat Robertson to Donald Trump, July 2017

When Pat Robertson interviewed Donald Trump for *The 700 Club* in July of 2017, the media turned it into a pretty big deal. After all, the President didn't do sit-down interviews, and while Pat was clearly in Trump's camp, the press was still trying to figure out how he'd been elected in the first place, so there were hopes that the interview would generate news.

The Huffington Post asked me to write a piece for publication the day after the interview. I wasn't surprised at what went on:

> Pat was clearly very much in sync with Trump's entire vision and government and predicted that he would be easily re-elected if he is able to get health care and taxation

under control. He reminded the President that thousands and thousands of Christians are praying for him, and will continue to do so.

Nothing presented here today was surprising or revealing, but it was a strong reminder of how far to the right we've moved as a country. Pat Robertson was and always will be a representative of the aristocrats, and he views life through that lens. As such, he has made the beliefs of the ruling class the beliefs of the gospel of self, which is a living, breathing dream for the politically conservative.

That those farther down the economic scale fully trust their "masters" is the single greatest cultural feat accomplished in the last 100 years or more, and it perplexes those who rely on education and reason. This is why I called the interview today "an important cultural moment," for if the observers continue to ignore this happening, more surprises will be in store at the polling places of America.

Pat Robertson's vision includes building an evangelical Christian "shadow government" that will eventually take over when the left completely fails. In Donald Trump, Pat has found his leader.

This wasn't an interview; it was a reverential hand job.

To embrace Pat Robertson's view of America under a God-appointed leader, a willingness to step outside certain realities is required—and that's exactly what's happened among evangelicals since Donald Trump was elected. Evangelicals must force themselves to look the other way as near-daily revelations about Trump's personal life, false narratives, and management style occur. Support him they do, and in words and ways that we cannot dismiss, for Pat's "shadow government" seems to now be coming out into the light.

The Washington Post's conservative commentator Mark Thiessen wrote that "Trump has arguably done more in his first year in office to protect life and religious freedom than any modern president."[34]

"Little wonder," he added, "that religious conservatives stick with him despite the Daniels revelations. This is not to say that Christians don't think a culture of fidelity is important. But the culture of life is important too. So is a culture that is welcoming to religious believers rather than waging war on them."

This motivator—the heartfelt belief that the Christian faith is under attack in our current culture—is one of the most important factors in Trump's support. So persecuted are evangelical Christians by a rotting culture, the thinking goes, that we need to fight back with everything we've got politically, rather than just give the nation over to the devil by saying nothing. During his campaign, Trump assured a salivating Christian right that "We're gonna bring it back," "We're gonna protect Christianity," and that "Christianity will have power if I'm President."

This issue of whether Christianity is under attack is complex and difficult to understand on every level. The parties involved have obviously differing views, but the arguments never really take place in the same contextual frame. One side argues that America was created as a Christian nation by Christians who came here to colonize in Jesus' name, while the other side argues that such a belief doesn't apply to the United States, because the country's founders were an eclectic group and wrote documents to protect citizens from rule by religion. Moreover, the Christian nation argument is irrelevant in modern times, because humankind has come such a long way in the last few centuries. One is a spiritual argument; the other is an argument of reason. One touts Holy Scripture, while the other relies on education and knowledge. One is upstream with the saints of old; the other is downstream in a hundred human tributaries. One believes the Bible is a "living document" while the other sees a certain anti-progressive rigidity in a set of archaic rules. One claims to argue faith; the other claims to argue logic.

Any reasonable, objective study of pre-Revolutionary American history makes a convincing case that Christianity was so enmeshed in daily life at the time that one must conclude its governance and institutions were filled with people of faith. Arguing against this requires changing history, although there's no real reason to do so. When English-speaking people landed at Cape Henry Virginia in 1607, their very first act was to plant a cross and claim the land on behalf of their Savior. This act is significant in that everything that follows flows from it, including the documents that recognized the potential for mischief in taking such a proclamation too far. Hence, we have the establishment clause of the First Amendment. However, that doesn't change the reality that the homes, by-ways, and communities of the colonies were filled with people of faith. Our democracy is based on oaths and promises that we make to each other, and there must be a form of punishment ahead for those who violate such that's beyond what the law can provide. Hence, we swear to tell the truth by putting our hand on the Bible in (some) courtrooms. Again, we can argue how effective it has been over the years, but this doesn't alter the history behind it all.

Moreover, any fair reading of early documents—including those of the Founding Fathers —can only be done using the language of the time, because the meanings of key words have changed over time. That means one must use the dictionaries of the era, Samuel Johnson's classic of 1755 and Webster's of 1828. When that is done, it takes considerable manipulation to conclude anything other than the truth of the claim that Christianity played a significant role in the formation of the US. It didn't need to be specifically spelled out, because it was assumed at the time. This in no way means America was birthed as a theocracy, but rather a country based on the belief that government "of the people, by the people, and for the people" meant that those same people were already self-governed through their faith. After all, it was John Wycliffe who first uttered the phrase when, upon completion of the first common English language translation of the Bible, he said, "This book shall make possible government of the people, by the people, and for the people." This is why those same Founding Fathers saw the need to include the establishment clause in the First Amendment. No single representation of God could never rule a people educated in the truths of the Bible.

As the country has become more secularized, therefore, it's been easy for Pat Robertson and other evangelical leaders to stir their followers over the actions of contemporary progressive thinkers. It forms the controversial pot within which the fundamentalists brew their self-serving anger, demanding a return "to the way it used to be." In this manner they became suckers for the flimflammery of a huckster in the 2016 Presidential election.

And progressives have played right into this longing for the good old days by visible actions that offer evidence of an alleged conspiracy against Christians. For example, who authorized academia and government to change our most basic calendar headings from B.C. (Before Christ) and A.D. (Anno Domini—year of our Lord) to B.C.E. (Before Common Era) and C.E. (Common Era)? There was no debate. No hearings. No input from others whatsoever. Suddenly, textbooks that our children used to study everything were printed using only B.C.E. and C.E., and all devout Christians could do was to loudly cry foul. There are also the matters of school prayer, the Ten Commandments, and the personal politics of gender. Is there a battle underway for the soul of the West? The answer is irrelevant, because the appearance of such a war is enough to make a political difference in the US. The fact, too, that progressives don't feel it necessary to argue the grounds of these complaints is problematic, because the assumption that it's unnecessary adds to the perceived arrogance that Christian conservatives use to argue their point.

Like most things in life, this is not black and white, for it involves a great many other cultural considerations. Moreover, the strict "Christian Nation" crowd deserves its own blame for gutting the fatted calf it now wishes to protect. Besides, the more important matter is that even if we agree that America was birthed among people who practiced differing forms of Christianity, what are we to do about it today? The wise answer is nothing.

Christianity is so divided into subsets that no one speaks on behalf of the whole. It's just not possible. Each denomination makes a case why its is the path to righteousness and an afterlife in heaven. Therefore, there really is no such thing as the "Christian perspective" we used to espouse back in my days at *The 700 Club*. Is that the Catholic perspective or the Protestant perspective? Is it premillennial or postmillennial? Is it Pentecostal or reformed? Liberal or conservative? Black or white? Judeo-Christian or just Christian? You can see the conflict, which is why the Establishment clause is there.

Therefore, by self-division alone, Christianity has lost its influence on the culture, and the voice that's complaining the loudest is the one that has the money and the resources to be heard, the white evangelicals, eighty-one percent of whom voted for Donald Trump in the last election. And so evangelical Christianity is the branch that is trying to drag us all in the direction of the theocracy the founders hoped to avoid. This is the group that has joined forces with the Republican Party—literally stolen the soul of the Republican Party—to make things happen that benefit their congregations. Of course, the GOP of the Reagan era was quite happy to invite this crowd into its midst, never thinking it would produce what we have today.

For these people, God apparently doesn't need our faith alone; He wants us to be a powerful political voice as well. This is the group that wants a war with Islam, because it leads to a premillennial one thousand years of glory in the name of Jesus. This is the group that needs Republican leadership in Washington to keep them tax-free and thriving, so they can recruit support from the mountain top of the one percent. This is the group that wants their prayer to be in public schools, their self-centered gospel to govern programs for the poor, their self-righteousness to dominate human hearts when it comes to personal medical or relationship decisions, their way of life to be the norm and to determine the nation's cultural mix, and their music, film, books, and art to be the only choice for all.

As my friend Jeff Jarvis said, "Sharia Law? That's nothing compared to Armageddon."

If there is but one truth about this particular group of Christians that should make us all wary, it is this: they will never be satisfied with just one victory in the culture wars. You can take that to the bank. As a self-governing people, we cannot and must not let our guard down. The history of humankind is littered with the tragedies of those who fell for idolatry, the promise of magic, and the fallibility of human nature. You want civil rights rolled back? Say nothing, do nothing today. You want women to return to the status of chattel? Say nothing, do nothing today. You want slavery brought back, corporal punishment in the public square, a culture dominated by fascist fear and bayonets? Say nothing, do nothing today.

From a historical perspective, there's a great difference between a culture being overthrown and one that self-destructs, which is what's really happening here. If, as the evangelicals insist, they were the ones who built this country, then its collapse must be birthed in the same womb. You cannot claim leadership for the one without responsibility for the other. This is the major blind spot of those who argue that the devil or the liberals or the communists or members of any other group are at fault. Therefore, positing that Christianity itself is the victim here is utterly self-serving, and it's also useless in trying to do anything about the evils around us. A slipping culture needs no outside help, if the ruling class within that culture cannot or will not accept responsibility for the slippage.

The ruling class in America today, we must now conclude, includes certain powerful and vocal elements from within the entire Judeo-Christian Western hegemony. The nobility of yesterday has been replaced by panting thieves for whom license, not liberty, is the desire demanding to be fed.

Past generations wouldn't recognize the Christianity that's "under attack" today, which includes truly remarkable claims and warnings from diehard leaders.

Author and Christian leader Mary Colbert: *He (God) works through the ones he chooses. We don't choose them. All we have to do is recognize them and when you recognize a chosen one and you have the discernment to know that they've been chosen and know that that's the will of God, then your life will be blessed. And if you come against the chosen one of God, you are bringing upon you and your children and your children's children curses like you have never seen. It puts a holy fear in me.*[35]

Newsweek: *The first Bible study group held for the US Cabinet in at least 100 years is led by a pastor (Ralph Drollinger, a pastor and president of Capitol Ministries: an organization which aims to "evangelize elected officials and lead them toward maturity in Christ.") who believes homosexuality is "illegitimate," who doesn't believe women should preach and has described Catholicism as a "false" religion.*[36]

Prosperity Gospel Evangelist Kenneth Copeland: *If Christians don't support Trump, they are risking the wrath of God. Trump has been chosen by God, and by rejecting him, they are rejecting God. They could be punished with barrenness, poverty, or even having a gay child.*[37]

The media generally doesn't keep track of statements like these and that doesn't help. As long as the press keeps religion—especially evangelical Christianity—in its "Sphere of Deviance," it will operate within a narrative that does not include the role of religion in the culture. This means the media operates outside the views of those for whom their faith is a working dynamic in their lives. This makes it impossible for reporters and commentators to ever figure out what really happened that put Donald Trump in the White House. They know nothing of the gospel of self. They're willing to discuss issues important to evangelicals, but they will always underestimate and minimize the importance of the faith's role in history and especially current events. It's simply not enough to cite ignorance and apply reason when reason itself is a proclaimed enemy of the faith. The problem, then, is that both sides in the great American split are debating on different playing fields.

Important questions are left out of the discussion entirely, such as the matter of whether Donald Trump belongs in the White House. Did God put him there, as the evangelicals claim? Trump has been in office two years, and it's gotten so that the only voices with good things to say about the man come from his own administration, a few extreme right-wing pundits, and the very core of his support, those evangelical Christians. He's made enemies of the press, his own party, and two-thirds of Americans, but to those who practice the gospel of self, these are all to be tolerated in the name of a God who has heard the cries of his people and decided to save the country. The gospel of self has taught Christians that they should be fighting in the political realm today for those who would restore righteousness to America and the world.

Let us now consider an argument that assumes the evangelicals are right, but alter the narrative just a bit. Perhaps God actually did put Donald Trump in office. Sometimes, the most likely and obvious answer to the question of whether something "should" be is its existence, and this forms the essence of the right response to certain evangelicals regarding the behavior of "their" man. Donald Trump IS the President, and to borrow the language of the faith, he's there because he's supposed to be there.

We must remember that evangelical fundamentalist Christians take their cues from the Bible, which they believe instructs them on how to respond to the cultural shifts in front of them. They're mad as hell and aren't going to take it anymore when it comes to morality, jobs, taxes, security, safety, freedoms, and education. It's no coincidence that these were the planks on which Trump campaigned, so it's easy to understand their excitement with the Trump candidacy. However, the Bible is filled with stories of people who stepped outside the will of God and were destroyed as a result.

If we can bring ourselves to ask why God put Donald Trump in the White House, the question follows: "What could be going on in the realm of the spirit in such a scenario?" The political evangelicals think it's to help them in their quest to fight against "sin" in the culture, to restore things to a time when life was supposedly easier or better. "Make America Great Again" fits this narrative perfectly. But what if the "sin" is within God's own people? Could

God be judging His own people and not the culture? Perhaps God is the One who's mad as hell and isn't going to take it anymore. Asking God—in prayer or otherwise—to judge the world can be a dangerous proposition, because the Bible clearly teaches that God's judgment begins with the "house of God," His people. This view is prophetic, completely in line with the teachings of both the Old and New Testaments. We only need to look at what Ezekiel said about Sodom to find prophetic parallels to today: "Now this was the sin of your sister Sodom: She and her daughters were arrogant, overfed and unconcerned; they did not help the poor and needy."[38]

Everyone knows there is a great divide between us in the West, one that life cannot tolerate forever, and perhaps that's what the Trump presidency is all about. Could our current chaos be the very path for resolving the great divide in our midst? Again borrowing from the language of the church, perhaps this is what God is trying to show us. After all, how often does life lead us through our own difficulties by forcing us to deal with them over and over until we get it right? If evangelicals can point to Sodom and its destruction (for homosexuality), then are we not able to use the argument above to refute that?

The rise of Trump is a false promise to those extreme fundamentalist believers who "just know" that he's right, because their church, their faith, and their families and friends all say so. It's a false promise, because truth is one of those things that has a way of surfacing no matter how many times people try to hide it. Life's way has always been to let humans do what we wish and watch as our efforts collapse. It's the hard way, but it's the way we learn as a species.

Our mistakes matter in our willingness to fulfill the potential of the human race. Could this be one of those times when we're able to fix some of the big ones? Pat Robertson and those of us who labored alongside him in the 1980s pushed and pulled the country to the political right in ways that were more brilliant than devious. He sincerely felt, and still feels, among other things, that the US would be better off with teacher-led prayer in schools, the Ten Commandments back on public walls, abortion returned to illegal status, the Johnson Amendment (prohibiting political involvement by churches) overturned, the inflow of Muslims into America stopped, and tax cuts that would permit the wealthy to give more to charities, including his own.

In so doing, Robertson wrote the strategy for not only Republicans but also for other evangelicals, which is why Christianity's brand is in so much trouble today. His influence cannot be overstated, because without the foundation laid by Robertson and *The 700 Club*, Donald Trump would never have been elected, and the country wouldn't be as divided as it is right now.

Notes

1. William Safire, ed. *Lend Me Your Ears: Great Speeches in History* (New York: W.W. Norton, 2004), p. 807.
2. Accessed on: http://shorensteincenter.org/conservative-media-influence-on-republican-party-jackie-calmes/
3. Discussed at length in Chapter Seven.
4. Daniel C. Hallin, *The Uncensored War: The Media and Vietnam*, (University of California Press, 1989), p. 117.
5. Jeremy Taylor, *The Whole Works of the Right Rev. Jeremy Taylor, 1856* (BiblioBazaar, 2008), p. 180.
6. Accessed on: https://www.aao.org/eye-health/diseases/central-serous-retinopathy-risk
7. Accessed on: https://hbr.org/2004/01/managers-and-leaders-are-they-different
8. Luke 6:38, King James Version
9. Accessed on: http://blogs.cbn.com/ChurchWatch/archive/2007/07/24/george-otis-sr.-another-christian-general-goes-home.aspx
10. Accessed on: http://www.nytimes.com/2000/07/30/magazine/george-herbert-walker-bush-the-accidental-vice-president.html
11. Accessed on: http://www.nytimes.com/1998/03/21/us/christian-broadcasting-network-to-pay-fine-for-its-political-efforts-in-1988.html
12. Ecclesiastes 10:4 (RSV)
13. Accessed on: http://www.gty.org/resources/articles/a124/christians-and-politics-part-1
14. *Evangelical Christians and Popular Culture: Pop Goes the Gospel*, Robert H. Woods, Ed. (ABC-CLIO, 2013), p. 67.
15. "As Contributions Fall, Robertson Lays Off 500 at CBN", *Philadelphia Inquirer*, June 6, 1987.

16. Danuta Pfeiffer, *Chiseled: A Memoir of Identity, Duplicity, and Divine Wine*, (Luminaire Press, 2015), 257.

17. Pfeiffer, 251.

18. Pat Robertson, *The Plan* (Nashville: Thomas Nelson Publishers, 1989), p. 178

19. Accessed on: http://www.nytimes.com/1998/03/21/us/christian-broadcasting-network-to-pay-fine-for-its-political-efforts-in-1988.html

20. Accessed on: http://www.fec.gov/audits/1988/Title26/PatRobertson1988.pdf

21. *New York Herald*, July 8, 1865 via http://law2.umkc.edu/faculty/projects/ftrials/lincolnconspiracy/herald78.html

22. Walter Lippmann, *The Phantom Public* (Transaction Publishers 1925), p. 145.

23. John Dewey, *The Political Writings*, 1993, edited by Debra Morris, Ian Shapiro (Indianapolis: Hackett Publishing, 1993), 248.

24. Accessed on https://books.google.com/books?id=dDQ0ScuSqNAC&pg=PA117&lpg=PA117&dq=sphere+of+legitimate+controversy&source=web&ots=SM5JzgByDk&sig=-Z_zvue3rT1PfuyNs8ulCR0S9Xw&hl=en&sa=X&oi=book_result&resnum=2&ct=result#v=onepage&q&f=false

25. Accessed on: http://www.hyperorg.com/blogger/2009/07/19/transparency-is-the-new-objectivity/

26. Safire, 805-11.

27. Accessed on: http://nationalreport.net/marcus-bachmann-refused-service-indiana-store-owner-assumed-gay/

28. Accessed on: http://speisa.com/modules/articles/index.php/item.1086/the-co-pilot-of-the-germanwings-airbus-was-a-convert-to-islam.html

29. Accessed on: https://www.facebook.com/AskDrBrown/photos/pb.109430102415934.-2207520000.1451396885./1149673721724895/?type=3&theater

30. Accessed on: http://libertyfirstnews.com/arrest-warrant-issued-for-black-teen-who-attacked-white-girl-causing-her-to-drop-baby-and-split-open-eyebrow/

31. Accessed on: https://www.youtube.com/watch?v=UXodRLLkth4
32. Accessed on: http://www.snopes.com/politics/obama/
    muslimreaction.asp
33. Accessed on: https://www.washingtonpost.com/news/the-
    intersect/wp/2015/12/18/what-was-fake-on-the-internet-this-
    week-why-this-is-the-final-column/
34. https://www.washingtonpost.com/opinions/why-conservative-
    christians-stick-with-trump/2018/03/23/2766309a-2def-11e8-
    8688-e053ba58f1e4_story.html
35. http://www.patheos.com/blogs/friendlyatheist/2017/04/04/
    christian-leader-god-will-curse-the-kids-and-grandkids-of-
    anyone-who-criticizes-donald-trump/
36. http://www.newsweek.com/white-house-bible-group-led-pastor-
    anti-gay-anti-women-anti-catholic-881860
37. http://allchristiannews.com/evangelical-leaders-warn-opposing-
    trump-face-serious-punishment-god/
38. Ezekiel 16:49 (NIV)

About the Author

Terry Heaton is a former executive producer of the Christian television news show *The 700 Club*, where he assisted Pat Robertson in his run for President in 1988, and where he was in a unique position to observe and participate in the development of the Christian right. A media theorist, he is the author of *Reinventing Local Media* and has written for media outlets throughout the United States, including *The Huffington Post*. Heaton plays guitar and five-string banjo and is a bluegrass music aficionado. He lives in Madison, Alabama.